D1367090

SELECTED POEMS

(1947 – 1980)

Courtesy of Harriette Stock

ROBERT STOCK

SELECTED POEMS

(1947 – 1980)

SELECTED BY DAVID GALLER AND HARRIETTE STOCK

WITH FOREWORD BY DAVID GALLER

**Crane & Hopper
Publishers**

Crane & Hopper, publishers
P.O. Box 234
Chappaqua, NY 10514

Covenants was first published in 1967 by Trident Press, a division of Simon & Schuster, Inc., New York, N.Y. Publication of *Some Signs Visible Before Judgment*, scheduled for publication, never materialized because of the author's death.

Acknowledgement is made to the following publications, in which many of these poems first appeared: *Aftermath, The Anagogic & Paideumic Review, Apple Street Anthology, Antaeus, The Ark, Athanor, Attention Please, Beatitude Anthology (City Lights), Blue Unicorn, Borestone Mountain Anthology (Best Poems of 1958), Chariton Review, Chowder Review, Coastlines, Contemporary Poetry, Contemporary Quarterly, Crazy Horse, Damascus Road (Dr. Generosity Anthology), Dramatika, Elsewhere, Extantis, Focus Midwest, For the Time Being, The Galley Sail Review, Glassworks, Glyph, Greenfield Review, Green's Magazine, Hika, The Humanist, Impact, Inlet, Light, The Little Magazine, Loon, Maple Leaf Rag, Michigan Quarterly Review, Midstream, Monks Pond, New Editions, New Laurel Review, The New Orleans Poetry Journal, The New York Times, Norte, Nutshell, Pivot, Poet & Critic, Poetry: a Magazine of Verse, Poetry London, Poetry Now, Quarterly Review of Literature, Renaissance, San Francisco Examiner, Seven Stray Cats, The Sewanee Review, South Dakota Review, Sou'Wester, Sparrow, Unmuzzled Ox, Wind, Works,* and *The Yale Review.*

Stock, Robert (1923-1981)
Selected Poems (1947-1980). Poetry.

Library of Congress Catalog Card number: 94-94207
ISBN 0-9640977-0-2 (cloth)
First Edition
10 9 8 7 6 5 4 3 2 1

Printed in the United States of America
Designed by Robert Jurgrau

CONTENTS

III

IV

From: COVENANTS (1967)

I

FOREWORD

Robert Stock, who died in New Orleans, Louisiana, in 1981, was born in St. Paul, Minnesota, fifty-eight years earlier. His mother, Freda Price, was a featured singer with the Chicago Opera Company; his father, a cattle buyer for the stockyards of that city. After his completion of the better part of high school in Minnesota, where he met his future wife, Harriette, the couple moved to San Francisco, where they were employed for the remainder of World War II at Marin Ship shipyard.

Of German descent, Stock had a lifelong fascination with the tropics, and, after a brief stay in New York City — where he contributed regularly to *Resistance* and *The Catholic Worker* — the family sailed to Brazil in the late 1940's, spending most of the four years there in Belém near the mouth of the Amazon. The poem, "To Tui . . .", suggests the reason for this journey, political as well as aesthetic; and the Stocks were, in future years, to live intermittently in Costa Rica and Mexico, attesting to their geographical preferences, as to an itinerant mode of living.

Stock always placed the writing of poetry first and, supported in this choice by his wife and later their five children, earned his living accordingly. The couple took what employment seemed least demanding; their standard of living was comfortable but extremely frugal. Never able to teach in universities because he lacked educational credentials or the reputation, say, of a Blackmur, the poet had early on read voraciously and had soon begun his Friday nights, at which a homespun, early version of the poetry workshop attracted writers wherever the Stocks settled, writers of every camp and ability. In San Francisco, for example, Marianne Moore, Kenneth Rexroth, Richard Eberhart, Robert Lowell, Philip Lamantia, Allen Ginsberg, and dozens of others crowded his flat on Friday nights; in New York, there were Paul Goodman, Julian Beck and Judith Malina, Spencer Holst, Irving Feldman, Jackson MacLow, et al. In short he developed, during forty years of writing, an underground renown as a teacher of versification; and the breadth and depth of his knowledge of different disciplines — languages, sciences, history, theology, philosophy — grew legendary in his lifetime. He was, additionally, an early translator into English of Carlos Drummond de Andrade, Mañuel Bandeira, Jorge de Lima, and Jules Supervielle, the French poet who emigrated to Uruguay.

In Brazil, Stock developed a permanent interest in the great Portuguese modernist, Fernando Pessoa. This poet had produced a separate body of work by each of five *heteronymos* or personae, each with his own style (ranging from Whitmanesque to Horatian ode) and own biography. The hoax always appealed to Stock deeply, who through the years was amassing a peerless technique along with multiple thematic interests, and perhaps the vastest and most compelling — to anti-intellectuals, repelling — vocabulary in the history of poetry — see the poem, " 'I'd Understand Yer Poemes Better . . .' " Pessoa's strategy, however, expressed itself differently in Stock. He did not — with one exception (below) — sign his poems with pseudonyms; rather, he kept writing in a number of styles ranging from vers libre to the formal, the ornate to the colloquial. This he did throughout his career. As early as 1954, he indicated to friends that he had enough poems, completed or in progress, for five or six book-length collections. Each volume would draw on poems in various styles, and these in turn would stem from the whole time-span of his writing. There was a wry and corrective humor at work, as there was serious intent. His one use of a pseudonym will illustrate the former. She was Rachel L'Estrange, a nymphomaniacal love poet, who submitted verses to Robert Bly's *The Sixties* in particular. The notes of repressed, pedantic encouragement of her "deep-image" explorations that Stock received from that quarter occasioned many moments of hilarity among the poet's acquaintances.

The present selection of Robert Stock's work comprises less than a quarter of his extant manuscripts and already-published poems, and the editor must take responsibility for the service or disservice done the author by this selection. *Some Early Poems* (Appendix) were chosen mainly, for instance, because the poet never disavowed them. Also, some are modernist curios indeed — "The Wandering Jew . . ." especially, for its verbal and astrological complexities. One is naturally curious — if one is interested in a writer's work — about his literary origins and divagations. While it is true that Stock's verse tended to become more accessible to the reader as the poet progressed, there were constant exceptions to the tendency toward plain-style expression.

All notes were composed by the poet, except for those pertaining to *Uncollected Poems*, which are mine, and are included only to assist impatient readers. The note to the poem, "Invisible Golden Sections," is taken verbatim from a letter sent me with the poem. It may well have never been intended for publication; but the fascination and amused delight I still experience on reading it caused me to include it. I have checked all words unknown to me in the 1971 edition of the OED.

We thank Jill Ligenza and Harold Holden for furnishing us with verses to which we had no previous access; our thanks, also, to Robert Jurgrau for his design and the preparation of this text for the printer.

David Galler
November 16 -17, 1993

UNCOLLECTED POEMS

(1947 – 1980)

I

HYMN DIRECTED SOMEWHERE TOWARD
THE PANTHEON

Whether partial or supreme,
in You some find their happiness,
others construe a gloomier scheme,
          some only guess;

to each the chaos-breasted tomorrow,
today the order turning stale,
to each his crime, to each his sorrow,
          corn under flail,

to all the harvest of their sense,
tidbits simmering in the stew,
for are we not Your preference,
          the height of You?

Yet most in depth I meet my soul
and from the flotsam seed my art,
for I can neither embrace the whole
          nor love the part.

SAXIFRAGE

Even on mountainsides
    saxifrage
prefers the cool north slopes.
    I like to feel
its leaves' deep-cut rosettes
    sting my hands
with winter strategies,
    I love to smell
the winter that's in summer.

SEVERAL LARGE ROCKS IN A SWIFTLY
RUSHING STREAM

That the stream should tremble
with timber and fern reflections
seems no less substantial
a fact than blood in my veins.
But what of the interplay
of sun and orange agaric
in whose tension each rock
shudders like a stage-propped
reality. It's somewhere
between El Greco's pure
stone transparencies,
so otherworldly,
and Dr. Johnson's proof
that experience is brutal
and nothing's insubstantial.
That somewhere's hard to place.
I'm tempted to call it blue.
But what of the ghostflower
with the hot orange blush
across its pallor, its face
lit by the rocks, its shudder
jellied in the hiatus
of a desperate rush,
lost in an ardent hush.

TRIADIC NODE FOR TIM REYNOLDS' DIGESTION

That the dialogue of pebbles and brooks,
that the monologue of sun and moon
are not hypostatic of history;
that the one and many tongues are hooks
to catch the betweens of multiplicity;
that poor fish gasp and thrash on bare-planked noon;

that history's the chance accumulation
of ruptured centers — light consuming light,
ditchwater energetic in stagnation,
or gormandize on acorns 'gainst the night;
that Cassiodoruses, when they busied be
in hiving, interrupt history;

that my patron, Saint Paulinus, sold
not his body to the barbarian
but history itself. Will we make bold
so to serve our ranker vandals? That
the shit is scattered before it hits the fan.
Yet gardener Nola blesses where they shat.

That, each man his own Cassiodorus, each
my patron, can, kenspeckling history,
convert subliminal magma to a peach,
his abature the substance of the shaw:
that change suspends the lycanthropic paw.
Conserve our mercies; that, or bend the knee.

THE RESCUERS

Not only through the dense bush cleared by fires
that do no prejudice to bud or leaf
while heating cold hard intellect in men,
but constantly in time the gods appear:
in white-eyed waves, in blue flame hovering
over the victor's head, the victim's mouth,
beneath an oitiçica's waxy leaves
the shadow, preternaturally cool,
that cost lovely Maria of the Sorrows
her maidenhead and name. I see one now!
Light on my shoulder, where I lost my wings,
he's stationed, pleasing less than guiding me,
embodied in a passion, thought, or song
when, in a crying need, assurances
of strength are heard. Just now I saw one flash!
Achilles, floundering with Scamander's fish,
dragged down by armor, at his brute despair,
entreated the gods. On one side looms Athena,
Poseidon to the other. Both his hands
are swept up by a vaulting harmony
while three are one in recognition deep
as what still clamors to engulf the man.
Make no mistake (as gods make no mistake):
the warrior is not hoist above his struggle,
nor prompt to haven where his spirit's not
the best-consenting cause of miracle.
Wordlessly, Achilles forges ahead.
The gods, the always-near-at-hand, are gone
as far as they are other, present now
in his strength and valor to gain the opposite shore.

9

PROMETHEUS PASSES THE TOAST

When I saw how man's spirit against his night
flickered, a thready fume of alcohol,
I knew that, come what would, I'd set that flame,
though I don't know for whose sake, night's or man's,

for, vexing the air, a spirit other than man's
ringed me with talons. So I seized the flame
whose venture lies in dissipating night,
and gave a form to wraiths of alcohol.

Denatured from the start, man's alcohol
was surely, every flask, as dregged as night.
It flared like fat, very like a man's
when, spitted on lust, his sweat is tongued by flame.

Was it only to grasp the nature of flame,
not to rebel, not to consume the man's
contemplation, pure, of alcohol?
What was it that I craved against my night?

Now it is all one flame. Here's to the man's
thin alcohol, while beaks besot his night.

DRUNKENNESS

for Carlos Franck

Sitting in a cantina, gin
and tonic in hand, the third, I see
above a swinging door the skin
of hard blue air around the mountain
change to a spreading bruise, the hungry

vapor hissing about my ears,
then darken with a stench of meat
till rancor glows in the dark. This fear's
a blackening sense my chest suffers
as warning with insistent drumbeat,

as pulse and memory. A cur
snuffles my traces. I undergo
who hunted my forefathers' fur:
darkness, genes and gin remember,
they smell the struck flint of the arrow

furrowing my cheek. I bring
a naked body to outrun
the quarry of my awakening
from ancestry, and my head, clearing,
denies the flush of hallucination.

Asylums of dawn! A dazzlement
of light that neither spins nor delves,
but comes to be so immanent
a skein, a membrane so transparent
that eyes in seeing see themselves.

WIND IN THE MIRROR

Not tornado I sing, not wind for wind's unruly sake.
The currents that blow in my mirror's face
are mostly gentle, scarcely a ripple
or dapple. Yet, this is not always the case:
a pucker has been seen to twist a lip,
a wry light vacillate across the lake.

They never seem to emerge,
they never seem to strike
eyes that peer into the eyes
that peer into the peering eyes.
If ever they did surge
against their glassy dyke
and focus all their force upon the brassy peers,
they'd fracture adamant for seven years,
a temporal for tears.

Narcissus, by the crash rudely waked,
stuck to his room like a burr;
Narcissus quaked
to think of what the gales might do to the furniture,
or what disaster areas, once set free to blow,
they might declare, or where they might elect to go.

Scheler's *pathos of distance* providently softens the blow.
But who has seen an oak twig driven through a wall,
half a red barn sailing the sulphured air,
or woke up howling with a bedful of splintered window —
no matter how many years ago —
familiarly will fall
into the unleashed terror of being there.

A warlock's curse, unlocked from glass,
accuses me. How can I pass?
Sir Inquisitor, was I
Prime Mover of the winds that devastated the middle American vast?
My eye
the disast-
er core?
A postulate of total responsibility
in a maieutic of total unity
assails me as it never did before.
Look! I am invisible in the vertical lake
that mirrors nothing but the wind's unruly sake.

THE CATHEDRAL

The tower's the thing snatching his cowled eyes:
a vertiginous gulf; but is it height or depth?
Up he scales by worn, precarious eyeholds,
down over breakneck roofs until a sewer
swallows him, secure in excrement;
but not to last. So swarms up bell-tower,
peering down, up, a martyr to rope and clang.
No way to organize the façade between,
no guild, no theology to profit flight,
a mole, gimlet-nosed, unsighted, frantic
to dig through the black tunnel of bright air.
Waiter, bring on the gin, the juicy soubrettes,
j'espérais la fin de la tête au coeur. . .
He crawls like a black ant on the bright stone.

SOLO FOR FOUR

Said Robinson, stone axe at a breadfruit tree:
"Which is truly alone? this timber? this me?"
The stone-edge answered: "Loneliness makes three."

Wuthered the tree: "I bear, so I know pain,
like you; I yield my pain, like you, in vain."
It crashed, so riddling: " . . . with me falls the rain."

Robbed acres recoiled: "Solitude's the stone
that feels fist-pressure after it's been thrown
and takes that stress as weightier than its own."

THE SPACE BETWEEN TWO BLADES OF GRASS
MEETS AN INTRACTABLE EGO

Bougainvillea purples burn
along the calm edges of sky;
dropped cashew-apples, rotting, turn
the breeze brandy where I lie
thinking of nothing, letting it in,
no challenge but to discipline.

Thrilled impositions of today
will not leave well enough alone:
tickling grass and its cricket say
I must account my shrinking zone
a prior loss, insist I cry
blue blazes at a yellow sky.

Remembering how God found Jonah
even in Tarshish, can I bid
the sacred precincts of Pomona
anesthetize my will amid
her labors, which ask nothing less
than I would yield to timelessness?

CERTAIN PRETEXTS

I've never seen such exigence
to circumscribe extremities
when nothing short of eminence
should bring this context to his knees.

He dared not venture near a mouth
without another in surmise,
he would not travel in the south
but take direction by surprise.

Once, deeply in love with beauty's own,
cohabited with her surrogate.
How, then, frequent the frangible bone
of all he fails to adumbrate?

When he remarks extremity
dwindle to fierce, bleak abstraction,
such is his consistency
that he supplants sum with fraction.

Abruptly here our text must end
to let his circum come unstanced
lest his unraveling should pend
till forfeit's own become romanced.

TO MY INEBRIETY

Old souse, how often, before head clears
    and I defray your wages,
I've bidden you numb my sensible fears,
    indulged your lust and rages,
your discomposure of piteous tears!

Yet always rush back to your bottle,
    swap insult with the boys,
detect the stubborn spreading mottle
    to sit alone mid noise —
a tiny figure, an open throttle.

For you convince me with your lies
    again and again, old souse,
how you'll forget (if I will) cries
    that have brought down the house
and how the richest silence buys.

THE PLANT CALLED YARROW

was probably brought to America
by some dank Puritan herbalist
half-afraid of it after dark;
a delicately hairy stalk
makes it Gorgeous George's flower,
and, conjured by it, devils bark
like man's best friend. To junkyards yarrow
imparts a casual grace, though few
would seed it near chrysanthemum;
and yet, I've had those small flat heads
of dull white blossom make me intone
Achillea millefolium
as though it were my styptic at Troy.
Called milfoil, stenchweed, thousand seal,
sanguinary, devil's nettle,
woundwort, bloodwort, carpenter's weed,
called field hops for the beer it brews,
old man's pepper for newfound fettle,
prevents baldness, relieves measles,
flushes kidneys and cures the toothache.
However, since the species used
for casting the wands is now extinct,
a principled *I Ching* scholar will leave
prophetic fancy disabused.
The more I think, the more I feel
for that benighted Puritan
subjected to a vegetable jibe.
His collar was probably askew.
Probably, he startled his years
by ending up with an Indian tribe.
Meanwhile, yarrow sometimes yields
a cluster with a rosy hue
to comfort disappointed seers.

QUEEN ANNE'S LACE

Whoever quite expected it would change,
blunt carrot fallowing back to origins,
no less? More adventitious than gelatins
left crawling up its stalk, how could its range
admit a residual past embargoed me,
me more, than more no less, whatever sticks?
Weeds now, they ride the fall while laden ricks
groan past, turnips a man's Penelope.

This off-white umbel with its near-black mole
if anything is lovelier now than then.
And, aired from the root, as subtle as again,
what a carrot-assault! I'll not condole
with wily Odysseus stinking in Circe's arms,
who dreamt I sliced the waves with barbarous fins
while in your own backyard your father's sins
possess the rankness and a garden's charms.

VARIATIONS WITHIN INSTANCES

When solemnly sentimental sanity
feels how difficult it's become to feel,
he packs his copy of Wordsworth to the country,
slyly romanticizing botany
to try the pinch of days on a liable heel.

In Madagascar grows the grapple-tree,
its seedpod a cothurnus of snarled fishhooks.
Under open, pulsating sky, a springbok,
capering, lands in the vise, a livery
to drag for acres of propagating ache.

Recognizing in the blissful face
of Caravaggio's *Death of the Virgin* that
of a ravaged whore just dragged from the Tiber's embrace,
the prelates, primed to pour, wink and displace
the "formal feeling" with mere requiescat.

Trapped in the drawstring muscles round the eyes,
the actual impinges: roads are narrow,
the shoe pinches, implications of sorrow
knot the heart to bleakest enterprise.
"Enough! Today I am your sole tomorrow.

Let me in to live at home in you."
No sooner wept than the wound scars over the breast,
debarring ingress to its only school:
itself. So grief, that pent-up Wandering Jew
from past the world, becomes the world's guest.

GRIEF

There's always the quiet, stupid grief
staggering in a vacant lot.
But stamping an upland meadow bare, a horse
is brought up short at cliff's edge;
its mane, as cumuli cover the sun,
is ashes on wind. If pity's prideless,
who is the hero who pities himself,
who hugs himself on the run? Putrefaction
separates yolk from white; the shell
suffers least. Those few brown stains
are food for thought. The hunger
dismounts and flips the reins to grief,
becoming its own too easy victim:
mouth's roof rubbed raw with ashes.
Water rises in the well, its brimming
ticks to the tides. Below, the children
pop bladderwrack. Their mouths explode
in silence thickened on silence.
It's like sitting in a perfect calm
and rousing with fistfuls of hair.

PART OF A TAROT FORTUNE

I pitched in the Tower, not yet struck
by lightning, at my right side you,
the High Priestess, and to my left
the Lovers tendering us the luck
of benefits that warmly accrue.
Intuitive power over events
was yours, a dominion that prevents
flames from forking out of the sky,
if it but will. Since we must lose
before we gain, you did not choose
the easier way: far better to die
and live impregnated by fire,
so falling into the threshing gyre
where spirit and body together fly

GRUNION RUN

for Arthur Boericke

Four nights after moon's full
I trudge out on a June beach
to bind the ninth wave's spell,
still thinking to pool meaning
from the ebbing seasons
aground in my veins; but catch
only slack waves tipped
with phosphorescence that turns
limpet, oyster and clam
inimical to man.

This is last of the year's
twelve nights when grunion spawn,
timed with the moon and sun,
just after high tide-turning
and just before the ebbing
— silversides, like brit,
each two fingers' span
in pairs scaling a wave,
riding the crest of my blood
on the almanac's pulsative.

When the comber shoals out
they scud along on sand,
where the runnel flows back
the female drills her tail
in the packed sand, and the male
clambers across her. They suck
alien air while seed

is buried and their trove
milted before the pair
escape by the next wave.

Do they have time to regret
the ninth wave? Two weeks only
are spared to hatch the roe,
helpless as plankton; then
a mad moon's higher tide
unsepulchres them to swim
home, fry, to the moon-warped sea.
Never a closer seed-hour
brings so many a hundred
unfathomably aware.

When my ninth wave's long spate
clambers from the windrows
of accumulation, may it
reel me in on its rush
and seed me deep in its crash;
for all the way home through night
I cast a school of shadows,
myself and the slippery fish,
in and out, half in depth,
enmeshed in untouchable flesh.

JACOB AGONISTES

Having survived my fill of wrestling at the ford,
    I've learned one thing: I've nothing more to give
that hare-lipped, stinking, matt-haired angel, since what I feared
    has turned, like my adherence, putative.

The angel, like my daemon genesis of a line
    to its own ends, lived by the stars, not sun,
and swore that its precipitates were mostly mine,
    I evenhanded, lopside-shanked, who run

from precipice to precipice yet never fall
    or if I fall can't tell the fall from flight.
I've nothing more to give, continuing is all;
    a bee-loud sun defends my crowning fight.

The failure wasn't God's, those years that he played dead,
    neither the angel's, and least of all my own:
there is no failure without a triumph in the deed,
    there is no flesh without impartial bone.

UNMAPPED ROAD

Half-opened, my door gave onto a long road
roaring in sunlight, hotter for the wind:
the lowly sill an inexhaustible goading,
the snake that took two lifetimes to unwind.

I thought: but what if the door were opened wide,
and crossing it quite as hard as the road's length?
Thought and would not stir: no galled outsider,
I sat and stared and gathered up my strength.

Before foot wandered or brow trailed in dust,
I followed the sun, considered my travels done,
yet never saw the road to me entrusted
so busy was I going a journey, gone.

CURRICULUM VITAE

In the middle of life I found myself
in the Holy City, where I divined
my cities to be but parodies
of the crucial force and polity
of this, which ends where it begins,
whose temples are the body of man
at the crossroads of possibility.
At the world-axis, accosting a man,
I asked him how to get where I
really wanted wholly to be.
He answered: "Two blocks straight ahead,
then turn left for two more blocks,
then right for one, right for two,
left for two and right for one,
right for two and left for two,
right one, right two, left two, right one,
and in that conjunction you will find
your inner believing's outward sign."
I didn't move because my mind
was One with the Holy City's design.

II

THE GAME OF THE THUNDERBOLT GODDESSES

1

The Golden Khan
of the Jurchid clan
has levied his horde
on the marches of the Khitan.
In a felt tent throned
on twelve great tigerskins,
he quaffs from a wolf's skull;
across his knees his sword
feeds on a hundred flames
while he and his cup trade grins.
It is a night for games,
for battle carouse, wild dances
that mime steppe distances
and blood & treasure unzoned
— all the revelry
of rapacity.

2

Six virgins painted
in primary colors
do the thunderbolt dance.
Each virgin juggles
six flashing mirrors,
thirty-six hundred flashes
with each breath taken
dazzle the eyes of the warriors
to each bared breast that jiggles,
each loin that thrashes
in time to the whirling mirrors.
These herders and hunters transform
horse-ridden inner-selves

into environment
by turning garden and farm
into an endless steppe.
They are beyond themselves
and almost immanent.

3

The crosshatching reflections
must mesmerize
but may not ever pierce
the great Khan's eyes
— or she will lose her own.
Golden only in name,
the Khan is stocky, flat-nosed,
bow-legged, with outsized
arms and head. His eyes entrench
deep in the high bone
gashed with scars. It's his stench
sets Khitan teeth on edge.
He is one with his race.
Shadows in his face
stretch as far and as far
as such whose habitat
is felt tents and such
as beat ground flat.

4

I stand at poet's distance
and feed on a hundred flames
to measure the dance
with each breath taken.
In the pasture of my mind
as in the steppe of his face
grass grows rank

now that the farm's forsaken,
now that the thing
I cannot abandon or find
glitters while devastation
makes me blind.

MITHRIDATES VI

Massive with gems, he bends aside
in surfeit from the viands and harp,
he toys with roses, not apprised
how every thorn is aimed at his heart.

Well-versed in the envenomed kiss,
he savors the poison, not the purge;
laboratory miasmas mix
with roses, cinnamon, and myrrh.

The royal surgeon, magnificent
a guarded thought below his lord,
drains off the blood his leech has let,
although the creature still absorbs.

That canny Mithridates should fill
his bowels with virulence was right:
a man whose heart has crowned him king
makes every rose a regicide.

BELLEROPHON AND THE PORTABLE UNIVERSE

Proetus of Argos gives his greeting's breath
to Iobates of Lycia: "Brother,
put the bearer of this letter to death."

And so the tried comedian bears the message
truly for each — our secret rictus, proof
that we be men, that manfully we do
our stretch across the plains of wandering,
human of humanshit, starry of starfall.
So sets off at a dash, as little aware
of omens and pledges of topography,
of milestones and surreal weathercocks,
as of the news he nuzzles like a plague.
So feel him sprinting, darker than all night
behind all snow, along the knuckled ridge
until the fist unclenches in palsied flats,
he driven by shrill fleas of insomnia,
sped onward by police and frontier guards
towards an incomprehensible sunrise.
Ha ha, hee hee! begun as twittering,
seedpods chattering in wind, as scabies
scraping a path, as whicker and gnashing teeth.
But fuzzy worms of silence curl in his ears,
eating our laughter before we laugh. It swells:
snickers with heads tossed back like stamping horses,
insisting with a hiss that swallows its snake
while adder-knots of entrails quake. His ears
dawdle in speeding feet. He trips over Lust
raping Love behind the rosebush, slides
on Compassion's vomit in the road, while Seemly
Maidenliness paws at his decorous fly.
Even his footprints are chortling: leaping ahead,

35

they rear up out of the dust and slap his shins.
Old Chaos, pregnant with the fellow he is,
aborts with laughter. Yet Bellerophon,
like any cuckold, is the last to know
why round him sides are splitting. Almost he smiles.
Arrived at Iobates' court at last,
guiltless before those eyes like oil on water,
that eagle perspective in the eyes of a crow,
he gives the letter into the tyrant's hands
and Iobates weeps because why not
and, losers keepers, both are bound to fail.

THE MIRACLE OF THE ROSES

I

Pass by! Stand from between me and my tree!
You take me, do you, for some chucklehead,
a ram to skip at the ragged parade of a skirt
tugged up to flatter ruts where brown legs clinch?
Try settling on a dog's-day puddle, you scum!
I saw you not a trice ago at the gate
wriggling for the Roman guards, I hear
their clipped coin chinking at your girdle. What
would any wild bitch out of Edom want
with my black windlessness and dust-rolled drought
—unless her sweat entailed some luckier wage
than nausea between two kinds of stone.

Draw a long look down to this fistful of dust,
a ram once, maybe, perhaps a centurion,
or one of those redheads, younger sons of God.
Could you, were you to welter in it naked,
raise its counted organs into lust?
Now look to me, to snarled and viscid hair,
to greening gangrene—no, don't touch me, girl,
just look! As simply as I blow this filth,
as scattered as it subsides, could any boy
from any of these starveling caravans
disperse me, so freely I've returned to man's
most elemental, least cohesive state.

But why's their mocking never till today
mined in me this vein? Their scowls I've known,
so eager to compound for worship, race

or surplus of my torpor. As if I cared!
I've undergone their jests: heard first at dawn,
by dusk garbled on more than a hundred tongues:
"Old Apollonius of Tyana's not
your master, which we plainly do perceive
by the frequency with which you break air";
they've dashed my pitcher with gall, or goaded their beasts
to piss up against me. Little it matters. Now,
after ten years sitting under this fig tree
waiting for lightning to strike a second blow,
they bait me with corrupt meat. Well,
I'll humor you and the captains, I'll prate awhile. In all
the stupefied sky there's only that one small cloud
clinging over the Mount of Olives now,
swollen like a she-goat's udder, and white;
but will lag westward after its color. Stay
until it drifts, reddened and storied, past
Jerusalem's Jaffa Gate. And stay no longer.

After all, I've still eye left for gauds.
I even know your name. Are you surprised?
Why, they hawk it out in the streets: "Mesha,
the young whore Mesha!" They say you spread those thighs
for twenty-five cutthroats a day and please
the last to sprawl there. Once — another jest —
right here at my feet you copulated, your trade
pelting me with stones till, thanks to you,
that moment came when men lose sight of pranks.
No thanks, though. I could have scraped you with my heel!
I could have dug my nails into my eyes,
stopped up ears, stopped mouth, and smelled you still!
Is it by choice you stink of camel dung
and two-legged goats? You women are but sacks

of excrement: to clasp you, have you burst
your steaming lusts in our arms — no beetle, I,
bent on a bloat! That you suppose your stench
peculiarly your own perdurable,
much more likely to evaporate
than to consume its victim, you in your sack,
I see. But have you dreamt exceptions? I know
your lot a glass that God could smash, or you
could choose to smash, if only you'd drink down
the wine that your first lover honored in you.

Though I'm aware that your commission here
intends to tar me in my nearest shame,
you move me, as if a cloud instead of mud,
you move me. Once we had a king, we Jews;
once a fat stream rejoiced the Vale of Kidron,
and then we had the king who raised this wall
and sighed more glory into Jerusalem
than Rome can screech in. Beauty like yours he sang,
while yet distinguishing between the temple
and venereal beds. He would have wisely learned
the way to praise the small and plumped and prompt
of the breast exposed to lure me from my tree.
I too could praise it, though the stream ran dry,
could grate out gravel with a flicker of gold.
The memory we Jews preserve in brine
falls longer, coldlier cut than all the shadows
across our sanctuaries in ruins. Black,
fruitless it may be, yet my fig tree's praise
has spanned you in its shadow for a spell.

Your conquering heroes, jealous for their coin,
have drafted the cloud that clocks our cheek by jowl,
and dangled it over the Mount to draw us out

in my rank temptation. Mesha, you, not I,
are close on change.
                              The captains often require:
"What's your sect, old fool, that you must stink
in the dead shade of a stick?" How could they know
how long my tree, parched as though it sucked
eruption from earth, has stood to our agonies!
My faith, like-manner, yields no figs; the limbs
crack, drop, not even fit for fuel. Listen:
do you or your sly captains really suppose
your breath tends fire enough to kindle mine?
'Twould be His most amazing—not His sweetest,
nor His bitterest, but most amazing—
miracle. Now may I tell a tale
to make you forget the captains?
                              My people say
the guardian angel of a newborn child
administers a fillip on his nose
to banish all celestial remembrance,
for, knowing what he knew, the world's career—
did he not forget—would drive him mad.
I wonder and have marveled that the mercy
of angels abandons the child before he's ripe,
before whatever it is consumes his ghost
become once more a child. One last enigma:
a woman crossing a lone graveyard at night
will out of convulsive dread conceive of herself.
Do you believe that? I can see your doubt
laugh along your throat. But now my chain
of rimes will tell you why this fabled tree
and I so bleakly share a wedded wait.

A five-mile mule ride south from Jerusalem
discloses my native town cresting a ridge
of limestone. You've heard tell of Bethlehem?

I loved it. Once I prized my privilege
of watching it turn midair from bone to flame
and float there, unconsumed, all but a bridge

from men to angels. The town welters in fame
for wonders — such as the Field Floridus.
I, too, that crucial day it won its name,

was present. Who was not there to discuss
the girl that they were going to burn at noon! —
a crowd of ranters, I as cantankerous

as any.
                Mesha, this is hardly the rune
you would have heard had I devised my song
upon the spot. Now my motives lie strewn

in dung from here to Bethlehem, a long
rough journey twelve years in the traveling.
Crushed meagre, hurled against the rocks, I wrong

my annals. Patience, and I yet may sing. . .
She stood adjudged of fornication. You
will scarce suppose her trespass anything

to trouble anybody save a Jew.
Our code's our skin. Her father, our judge, held high
authority, so total submission was due

his rigor which (though she was vouched to vie
with Ruth for beauty, and stood, till then, supreme
in stature of virtue) ruled that she must die.

You shudder, Mesha? Stand. One heightened seam
secures the robe in which you're both revealed.
Shudder, Mesha, and when you needs must, scream.

That far, you're twins.
                        At noon the tyrannous field
exhaled a kiln where limestone ached to melt
to quicklime. If the squat sky was sealed

in brass, the ground of our assembly felt
like iron scorified in the thronged demand
of untold executions. No one knelt

there ever, neither priest nor victim. Sand,
what little there was, crept over the slab like lice
in the sullen sorry gusts that stir that land.

A nearby watch of almond trees, precise
with gleamings of acacia, seemed a mile
in haze. The sun clanged, hot for the sacrifice.

I stood at the crowd's edge, eyes lowered, and while
an elder spouted official casuistry,
I heard a hundred hands hurry the pile

of sticks waist-high: dead wood, but still to me
fragrant of blossoms crushed at the girl's pink ear.
And then I felt the chill piercingly

and, looking up, I saw the sunrays veer
together, converging on her, deserting the route
of sightseers. She seemed crystal, a bright spear

struck upright from the ground. Her pride's redoubt
rose staunch against the priestly purpose — and yet,
their puny bundle of faggots would thaw her out!

My pulse stopped, eyes stopped, ears stopped, while the threat,
the imminent harrier, frayed the edge off fear
and platitudinized the tragic sweat

which dips the body in its brightest tear,
imposing petty apprehension instead:
unmanned by snakes in wells, the emptied wier,

waylayings after the feast, lost maidenhead,
dismay, distrust, panic; uneasy, tense.
The torch! and wind, on a red wing bursting, sped

Gehenna's worms writhing into dense
wreaths at her feet. She cried out, parting the smoke:
"A sign, my God! Give them my innocence!"

And they, the others, mocked her to provoke
some slightest rancor: "Yes, a sign to breed
virginity!" Out of what desert she spoke

I've never fathomed, yet it didn't exceed
my own before her cry set her alone.
My spine uncrooked. I plundered for my creed

self-generous cynicism — to match her own!
And I recalled how golden were her thighs
when any breeze (wanting to be shown)

would ruffle their covert hairs. How strange that her eyes,
or all our nights together, hadn't prepared
me for my mistress in this outrageous guise!

Charred flesh I owed her none. But shortly there'd
be stench to cope with (as once in my boyhood
when lightning struck my elder brother and spared

my father but me), and I'd go sick. Black wood
rushed red with legions of contending rage.
(Scream now, Mesha, such being your livelihood —

to scream. Those flames, each painstaking swage
frostily mirrored in the multitude's eye,
smoulder in yours. Now scream — or never! That page

burns black and skitters far beyond your cry.)
The smoke's fog vanished in a sun of wonder.
Flames, the first that stormed against her thigh,

fell back, while odor that took shape from thunder,
concluded in roses, petals everywhere.
And she, she stood forth, chains and time asunder,

as the moon at mid-day stands upon the air,
her body transparent in that light of roses —
yet each thorn leveled at me quailing there.

My pores grew eyes to see what still opposes
quiet in me; and all that crowd, that mas-
sive bellows, fell silent, as a dream discloses

thunder in images; but I, alas,
waking, feeling her eyes on me. And, knowing
she saw right through me, I was cold as glass.

3

The song is over, the chain broken. Here
also talk should end—or break, for who,
except a dead man, can be cold as glass?
Her? As for her, I do not know. I fled
that Bethlehem for this Jerusalem
and dropped all further knowledge by the way.
Perhaps she bore our child. Or crumbled perhaps,
afterwards, in doubt. Or secretly burned
the rest of her days. Did I describe her? No.
Not even as she stood imploring God?
My song was not entire; it made no song.
Still, let me ramble on awhile. Don't go.
Our cloud frothing over the towers will do
for topic. Stay awhile. Your back, so thin
and sorrowing now, troubles my tale. Are you
afraid of me, more by a song appalled
than by the stench around my chosen tree?

Upon that miracle a second thrives,
though to what end it swells this monstrous me
exceeds my wisdom. Has my summer wronged
my wintry sense? Did Adam, when he fell,
seal the glory and science of Solomon?
Does the angel's double-witted sword
mirror Job's reunion with his God?
This parasite, myself, is meaningless
until what flourished *there* is garnered. Did
the body-scripture of that paragon
illuminate her wisdom in such color
that Someone through pure marvel had to do
something? But, as for God, unless I freeze
outside nature, I can never be sure
the hand that delves me to the quick is His.

45

While yet a boy, I heard my father, a priest,
conversing with a friend on demon lore,
how unseen evil or its fallen doers,
sons and daughters of giants in the earth,
gather human seed and of it mould
human counterfeits permitting the gift
of tangibility. What if the seed
I spent with her, the woman not being human,
was shed in Onan's waste — into her power,
and not into a fructifying womb —
in short, the starcrossed circumstance no less
than inexpiable phantasmagoria?

Always caverned in my skull this thought
turns roses nightmare; even my tree, in vain . . .
Stretch out beside me. Our cloud, our subterfuge,
has swept well westward now, and a wind from the sea
has quickened so many to meet it I can't tell
ours from the strangers. Look, how all return,
darkening and piling up in force.
Our prophet Daniel warned we must expect
the Messiah on a stormcloud, never an ass.
Lie closer by and let me stroke your arm.
Like this. My queries importune no answers . . .

Were there antecedent events, unknown
to observation, to constitute those roses
not miracle but natural event?
Conversely, it was miracle if the effect
exceeded possible means. I've laid the dust
of such gratuitous enigmas for hours
while sitting here as like submissive rock

as mind can will; but I have ears, mouth, eyes,
winds never lack to rise, to pierce my sight,
to blind my soul with images: veiled women
gliding through family graveyards in a dim
blue mental light; the forms of fire — so many!
Why, common blushing (oh, whatever cause it)
can swarm that dust like wasps about my head.

Your arm's the smoothest thing that I have touched
since I touched flowers last. Make no attempt
to understand my ravings. Behemoth,
whose breath sets coals on fire, blows so hard
in my mouth that corpses, buried since my prick
was buried in the thought of a thought of a dream,
come struggling out of the brimstone pit of me . . .
Forgive me, Mesha. Despite your trembling hands
I was about to call you whore again.

The urging of my hand along your arm
is act, not episode: no pentecost
depends upon confusions entertained
twixt dove and jackdaw; nor fire and water . . .
nor roses.
                    Yes! those roses were bestowing
their sum history on presences that pass:
eternity revealed in time, and glowing.
I touch you and the link is clear as glass.

4

(Marius to a comrade in the guardhouse)
Go fetch me a dry cloak, boy, and mull my wine,
three cloves — and mind! no cardamom at all.
That done, scrub a burnish on my sword.

Hop to it, boy! I tell you, Pertinax,
we've got to keep these Jewboys running ragged,
or stomp they'll come down on our toes. With luck
he'll botch it, jumble cardamom and cloves,
and if he doesn't, I'll stand my ground he did.
Either way, he'll sleep with the flat of my blade!
Another hour of this rain and we'll pick figs,
not curses, off the old man's starkstone tree!
About the gaffer, though. Perhaps the rain
and lightning took to playing tricks on my eyes,
but our own trick has miscarried; and worse,
somehow carried. Jewboy! hey there, Jewboy!
mull a rose in my wine and mull it quick!
Well, after sending the whore, we watched their gab,
his at first with a rage on. Guess he figured
this as Operation Kid the Goat.
He didn't send her packing, though, but fumed,
fumed and gossiped. All the while she'd nod
her yeas and nays, then rile him up again
with arts too clumsy to debauch a toad.
Isaak the Elder's daughter "happened by"
and stopped to air her tongue. I'd say she heats
a goblin twixt her legs, though still virgin
likely enough. She hung around till dark,
then scuttled, but not before Rufus bagged a free
feel — so figure she'll be back for more.
The upshot? Well, we'd all forgot the can
that we had tied to the old bastard's tail.
It turned as black as an Aethiopian's bottom;
rain came bucketing down. I stood my guard
alone because we had dismissed the men
when we'd got started fooling with the wench.
You can't treat that kind as you would a Mesha.
Lightning was running amuck when my relief

showed up at last. I marched down to the tree
to check results, fully expecting to find
the slut run off to hovel with some herdsman
and the old owl, as always, rain or shine,
with his scabbed back screwed into that treetrunk.
As I came near, the lightning's glare outlined
picked-over bones: his tree's white carcass. Oh,
I didn't see all that, of course. A moment
it lasted, that was all. And yet I'd swear
rain hissed off wood as blood off a hot sword.
And then, as darkness lowered again, I saw —
you'll never believe it — under the tree I saw
them at it, foul and slimed in dung and mire.
I thought at first that he was killing her.
You must remember, Pertinax, our way —
not ours, but our command's, when in the north —
their way of slitting a native woman's throat
just at the culmination of love-play?
Not many traits of that Hyrcanean murk
seem quite as fitting here so near to Rome.
I wasn't afraid. You know my battle-worth.
But I was hesitant, slow to react:
anything might lurk in all that filth!

So I poked them with my sword. Not hard,
but shoved it tolerantly between their bellies.
Quicker than zut-zut she was up and off,
a streak of phosphor as far as the Horse Gate
where she flickered into the valley and vanished,
running naked into the south, but whether
in joy or agony I couldn't guess.
And the damned Jew was sprawled in ecstasy,
blue and kind of shining as though he'd gorged

Gehenna's flames — as ancient as their race.
I thought the lightning flashed from him, I did!
That wasn't part of our joke as it was planned.
Even our coins were scattered among the rubble.
Well, that whore's gone, though she was middling to good —
piggish, though. Anyhow, who'd tup her
now — unless to serve her as we served
the Scythian maidens, huh, Pertinax?

It's all the same. Look, we've got our silver.
Managed to retrieve them from the mud.
And, brother, how we'll get his goat tomorrow!
Oh? You doubt if he'll be there tomorrow?
You're right, of course; and even if he stayed,
our joke's gone sour, for he's turned wild and mad.
The world, he howled, was glass, instant with lightning;
exulted he'd been struck by fire at last
and smelled, he babbled, of roses. Yes, our joke's
turned sour, for he, gone mad, is therefore holy.

AMBASSADOR FROM INDIA

Caesar Augustus, as a matter of course
initiated at Eleusis, and not
himself without his kind's ambition, bade
the mysteries celebrated out of season
and conscience, staging the phanes' raree-show,
yea to the very epopteia, to please
Zarmaros, Brahmin ambassador, as though
our Chief of State ordered the Rose Bowl Game
played in August for the Maharaj Ji.
The Brahmin, moved by pride and arrogance
to mend the rite with public demonstration,
immolated himself in the flaring up
that for a millennium had been Athens' awe.
He did not change the rite, the rite changed him;
the blaze died down as it had always done.

ASHES ASHES ALL FALL DOWN

> *"We were hiding in a hollow when the blue wolf*
> *instructed his grandson, Jenghiz Khan, in the*
> *black science of germ warfare; we were disguised*
> *in furs when the plaguey dead were catapulted in-*
> *to Kaffa; we stowed away our souls on the three*
> *ships that brought the infection home; and through*
> *many centuries we have smiled fondly at the simple*
> *rimes of children, though our nightmares inter-*
> *pret them aright."*
>
> — from *The Journals of William Selkirk*

Furred sons of the blue wolf slant-eyed rode from the east,
catapults drumming into our citadels
their wide bubonic brothers. Rat's-bane cells
black-ringed the rosy for a trophied feast
while three dynamics of catastrophe
slipped moorings to Genoa, whence imposthumous bloom
pinched Europe's pockets with a prolonged perfume —
man's fate patrolled in the tight gut of a flea.
Behold the man! who from a bareness pricks
boils on the holy town, yet from whose side
compassion will not pluck the crab or worm.
Have you got stomach for our politics?
Mastered by our cargo, we nourish the germ
that blistered the cities that blacken the bodies that died.

SIGISMONDO MALATESTA BRINGS HIS FAVORITE
PHILOSOPHER'S BONES TO ITALY

With horses' hooves clattering
and armament's jangling,
we climb the bent, cobbled streets

at dead of night. I tighten
my knuckles to keep
lightning in my fists,

round every corner thinking
to clash with the pious rage
of Federigo, Duke of Urbino,

Urbino of these grim mountains,
while mine's the smiling coast
from Rimini north and south,

but mountains also mine by right
seignorial (despite disputes)
and the bare thought in these bright bones.

Our torches flicker and flare
on whitewashed walls,
quitting them twice as black

behind us where the townsfolk
quiver abed. "A citizen
of hell," Aeneus Sylvius

(who burnt me in effigy
at Rome) declared me, and
(against my Alberti and Duccio

Urbino can only muster
the geometry of Piero
and Pisanello's glooms)

"the scandal of Italy."
Thus Urbino, looking for brimstone,
will find an ammoniac trail.

From war against the Turks
I bring back, if not
the pope's caecal victory,

Gemisto Plethon's bones
in their narrow silver casket
shining in the dark,

which I'll lay next Isotta's
to coin the union of thought and love,
outraging His Holiness, leaving Urbino
to dicker and drool at ducks and drakes.

LOUIS XI

There was one hour in which the Middle Ages
    at a blow were over, damsel, book and spire.

He grasped for time sweet time at gravel and thorn
    while princes hid it in close ambages
of mail and broad-sleeved samite. There it staled,
    rustling fainter till it expired
in perfidy. God's grace! afoot he'd go,
    his sole demesne a beggar's bowl,
in buff and dun as was his wont to fare,
    and sound the folk. Answered no sound.
A shriek, from spittlehoused Villon's throat torn,
    was silent as Our Lady's choir.
While pincers crawled on Louis' flanks, on Paris,
    his faith in negotiation failed,
and with faith youth. There was no middleground
    either side the ravages.

Within the hour his eyes are hard and veiled.
    From age the Renaissance is born.

FOUR INSCRIPTIONS FOR THE SUNDIAL OF A LOST
RACE OF POLYPHEMUS

1

They wonder as they ripen:
will the bent bough break before they fall?
If love be ripe, time is overripe;
the cherry from within
will be riddled open,
the bough be forgotten.
This, of very function
requited my erect gnomon,
is what I dote on most of all.

2

You call that a picnic? A rainy haze
always just beyond the beyond,
behind the Pleiades, behind the eyes
that lie below or upon the damp grass?
That was no picnic at all! The crows
nearly drowned in crossing the Hyades
and the red tick fell struggling awalt
to drop below the bruised horizon.

3

The shadow, as ever, moves,
but seems more piercing now.
Fine lovers there are none.
Perhaps it's better so:
feel it? feel the shadow
sweeping across the sun?
Squirrel and oak are sick:

antidromous, azoic.
I crave to hear the minute
crumbling of soil round the root,
blades in their growing babble,
the bronze-belled fritillary
straining to droop toward me,
not, not this interminable
tick tick tick tick tick tick

4

Now I lay me down to night,
out of mind when out of sight.
If I should break before I wake,
pray to the moon — for God's sake!

GO AS PLAYED IN THE BEST CIRCLES; OR, ROTTEN AXE-HANDLE

●

Life's a many-dimensioned game of go,
submits a fellow scribe. I'd recommend
to my companions of the subtle board
a pervious antiperistasis: for life's
a beginning and end surround by its middle;
for life's an acrobat whose pratfalls show
wholly aleatory, a partial riddle.
Beginning's all, beyond that all is end,
each active through the middle's taut accord,
according to this ancient game of go.

○

In the woodcutter's blood the woods awake.
His nostrils augur the middle of next week
whose chips and resins itch for his new blade.
Crocus and primrose, the season's indulgent blood,
congeal underfoot, and down through the tops of trees
flashes of sunlight, coming and going, surprise
daybreak in lifting dew and on shook leaf.
A cuckoo's call-note melts away in a laugh.
But when the clearing of his own cutting appears
(that solitude whose prévenance depures
his veins), his blood rushes all to his head.
In the bright clearing, there where nothing's hid,
two youths, like psychopomps, so waxen and grave,
over a board bend brooding. There they strive
wordlessly, no turmoil, tears nor sweat,
and one snaps black stones down, and one snaps white.

Unconquerably setting himself in the sun
of this initiatory moment soon
to fade, he leans on his axe-handle, rapt
in vision, too wonderstruck to interrupt.

●

When angels guide us out of time,
what but our souls do we overtake
as patterns form, transform, compound
in gradual neat encirclements
that pardon us our perfidies.
In this sublime,
new achievabilities,
crystal-strict, past accidents,
embrace the life their forms surround.
And so black forfeits for the sake
of design becoming paradigm.

O

Surprising the crisis, always just at once,
the axe-handle buckles, giving up wood's response
    to gravitating rot. The woodcutter,
tumbling to the brown leaf, blinks up at the Great Bear.
    The youths have vanished. On a stump the board
awaits. A hero dreaming of hell — so goes the story —
    plucks there a flower, wakes with it in his hand.
Our hero, dreaming of life, has like an angel passed
    how many acres burnt out by his soul
and wept to watch the deluge bring the green back home.
    And so he fashions black from earth and fire
and from surrounding sea and air he brings back white.

EPISTLE TO PRESCOTT S. LIDDELL

I'm writing from the hinterland, a block
more or less from Times Square's hell. Dumb Stock
has domiciled on Mexico's wrong coast,
duned Veracruz, where he with Hart Crane's ghost
communes. As one who has not time for time,
you deprecate the banjo and the rhyme,
yet strut the unlikely text for more than one
probe for secrets where perhaps are none.
Okay; let's make it like our go games where the fun
lies in surrounding to pounce. Your neighborhood
connection for cheerful-little-earfuls would
inform you (though it leave you more frenetic)
that alcohol's been found a carcinogenic.
I won't — and yet just did. You hardly deserve
so sly, insidious an inside curve.

From Ithaca to Pakistan to Rome
you've never trudged a furlong from your home.
Yet on you roam, the bussed somnambulist
of hither and yon, no anthropologist
turned up missing in jungle or academe
but too transmigrant in another dream,
and, self-bestirred, exhibiting the wiles
magicians cherish: now you see the miles
and now you don't, both near and far destroyed,
with logorrhea rummaging the void.
Rites of passage, and sacrificial, too,
your rich blood, spilled, collects like morning dew,
and rides the observation car to Timbuctoo.
Your silence teeters a second. Then Kyoto,
Matto Grosso, Chittagong, and Quito,

Gnome (for you can reconstruct a place
into yourself and still regard its face).
A tourist trots to say that he has been,
but nothing sees, too busy being seen.
You flee the tourist and the privateer,
the bailiff, borderguard, and phony seer,
though happily you are no cenobite.
Those driven myths of 1950's flight
who trouped under Neal's capsuled buskin of speed
wound up unwound, yet couldn't quiet a need
that never touched the ground. That's not your case.
Hanging no hat, you guard your sense of place.
Meanwhile, that suitcase never in twenty years
wholly unpacked stares up into your fears
of stasis, blinks, and mumbles, "Your last ditch
unless you get a gig or marry rich"
or learn to conjure distance like a witch.
Who cares that you have wandered far, Liddell?
Our care is that through hell you've traveled well.

THE FLABBERGASTING OF THE TRUE
& FALSE BASILISK

Don't hoot at the poor dear basilisk,
don't snicker aloud as he minces by,
     born all in the land of Cockayne, O.
When chanticleer laid him ye dogstar was high,
and lifewise he, hatched seven years
     by granny toad in a sty.

Although he had letched for no odalisque
the gods had not paid him his unicorn,
     he trowed in that land of Cockayne, O.
Since lads in John Tzetzes did, he'd adorn
his figure in jupes, his features in leers
     he'd await the ravishing horn.

Smoothing his lap with a flirt and a frisk,
he camped out under the nutmeg tree,
     perfuming the land of Cockayne, O.
Soon, breakneck from the canebreak, see
what rural, what cuddly rhino nears,
     comes, rolls with him wantonly.

Here, beneath the skirts of earth,
lies the quaint queer basilisk.
O thou pilgrim through Cockayne,
pause and marvel at great worth
brutely subject to mere girth
and morte before his prime, at a whisk!
     a stain on the vast inane.

SIR JOHN MANDEVILLE AND I SAT UP LATE TALKING

Wander, you may wander
farther than Prester John
and yet wind nowhere: this concerns
not self-discovery but
poetry: beholding yourself
not on a bare hillside
but in some Garden of Adonis.
Each moment as it comes
sets forth what you know.
It comes at once: I know
this orchid for the parasite
it is, these fire ants
streaming up and down a trunk,
down the word, up the poem,
a final life no less
epiphytic than the moon's,
leaving all the ten thousand
routes to Jerusalem
alone in the dark; I know
well it is this I know.
How long is a problem only
to last year's calendars.

Later, recognize
a whole, once a sequence
finally a whole, and not
electric to light
receding halls of fame,
but dumbfounded — Moses,
the burning bush.

A VOYAGER TAKES PAUSE

Sweating grinds, we stoked the boilers,
Blaise Cendrars,
slipping by the forefinger capes
we sailed into different Guanabara Bays, you and I,
even though from our respective decks and dates
both of us must have sung out at sight of the same palms,
their scrolled surf steeper than masts,
up there like so many cockeyed Peters swerving aside,
denying the sea, denying the land.

That I establish this between us in pristine detail
is essential, though perhaps no more than ritual — I don't know.
I know that later, at a bar, I likened them to disheveled coronals
confounded with inconsequent handkerchiefs fleecing a grey dawn
and laughter clicking like a pingpong match where everybody loses.
That's how I threw them out of joint, those palms.
Now we may observe them as they were and are,
ablather and lissome, even to their coconuts restored,
as though we sat us down together and belted cachaças

or maybe vodkas. Let's accordingly assume
that the Kremlin you once etched in snowy words
did resemble the witch's cottage in Hansel and Gretel.
God has granted me but skin and bones.
I could gobble down those verses, almonds, icing, bells and all.
And yet they are not fattening, for good or ill,
and how adroitly we are pimped into the perception
that *La Petite Jehanne de France, en ce temps-là,*
would cleanse any Augean stable of a bed she happened into.

Vodka's bruin brew
and cachaça's little better. Nevertheless,
I'd like you to meet Jacaré, croc in hide and tenacity
who, though hardly a match for your *voyageur en bijouterie,*
certainly confers dignity on cachaça.
Following each of seven bouts with his Stepmother Malaria
came diamond fever to steal him back into the jungles of his silence.
After him (into that welter of assassins, redskins, wreathing snakes,
        great sunburst of cats
and that *lontra* flashing murderously at his best friend's throat
and dragging him under just when he'd found a magnificent diamond)
I could not follow, neither really fail to follow.
Jacaré! You would've liked the assassin. He'd've idolized you.
He postulates a kind of kindred ken between us.

But Guanabara Bay!
Where over blonde waters butterflies came flickering
to meet and greet you
to me was given the high, methodical carousel of carrionbirds
blackly programming the bonewhite pile of *Port Déception.*
What was bony in the heart I brought to bear?

THE SELECTED POEMS OF MAÑUEL BANDEIRA

While still in the bookshop on Rua Carioca,
before the pages were cut, a pair of bookworms
enjoyed my copy of Bandeira's poems.
The first small puncture occurs on page 69,
lower left-hand corner, where a savory
"Ballad of St. Mary Egyptian" proved
too strong a temptation to let pass.
On page 97 a second bookworm
(hereinafter known as Joe) appears,
a little to the right and up the page.
At "Family Boardinghouse," page 103,
Joe begins a boldly elongating journey
toward Josie, the primal worm, until they meet
on page 127. A mystery develops
at 141, a separation whose cause we may infer
from the more melancholy poems; whereupon Joe
declines and vanishes at 152.
Bravely on to the end goes Josie,
though by the Table of Contents she's no more
than a pinprick. Beyond the book,
beyond Rio de Janeiro and Brazil,
here in the symbol, she too disappears
like the urbane and witty conversation
of Mañuel Bandeira, now a memory
in the eaten minds of a few old men.

III

BATTLE SCENE

A technical scandal in its day,
a moral ambiguity in ours,
Uccello's *Battle of San Romano* flowers
  across the ages, but won't stay
our present predicament, nor tell us why
man seems to change his mind but never his eye.

No matter how cold the eye, it revels
in a host of details that one by one appear
out of the whole design, until it's clear
  the whole conceals what it reveals.
The pattern of shattered lances on the ground
imply in martial trumpets a fugal sound.

Order from chaos: Goya preserved
some chaos to appease his moral muse;
Uccello let his form's perfection accuse
  disorder, while each corpse is nerved
beyond the uncontrollable life that compares
soldiers so helplessly with horses and hares.

INVISIBLE GOLDEN SECTIONS

Ghiberti's great door keeps his Adam immured
in a bronze dream, no in, no out, secured
to woman, separation now assured
in private perspectiveless oneiric space
that on all sides brushes the dreamer's face.

The public widower inherits tears
the widow in secret sheds, yet never hears
his mind's mazy motions changing the years
back into feelings she cannot have known.
One farther step and you will stand alone.

The furniture, divided in its turn,
declares for widow or widower. To yearn
for chattel and goods is not a bed's concern.
A word, unspoken, shouts their clamor down
and sheer replevin falls upon the town.

Adam's rib sticks in his throat for lack of love;
Eve goes dim-sighted and cannot witness above
the fog. Divorce of water and land, of dove
and serpent, paradigm the widow. June
makes no pledge that we will see a moon.

Division tempts you into solitude.
Then follows frenzy, then an interlude
of meaning starved for understanding's food.
The tempter holds my breath; I'm thick with thieves.
Minutes are just so many thin reprieves.

WHEREIN THE MAKER'S RIGHT HAND MORALIZES THE WAY TO A FAMILIAR BUT RARE FELICITY, WHATWHILE THE LEFT HAND SEEMINGLY KNOWETH NOT ITS BROTHER'S AMBAGES AND SO FALLETH IN THE WAY OF AN UNDISCERNING SUBTRACTION

Driven to my shelves for Plato, aware
for months that Plato held this hour in store,
groping for the tome, I surprised my hand
splayed against the windy bookscape, lo!
the Golden Mean in sweet particulars
of human architecture: 2 to 3
and 3 to 5 — the 5th and major 6th!
I'm hardly disappointed, then, to know
hand and ankle-bone and spinal stave,
parts of the same whole and soul, are 3 to 1.
How sweet a subsistence stores how starry a truth!

Yet something amazes: that we cannot thrive
on the candor of our proportions. For our roots,
dithering in the anemocracies
that, adding 2 and 2, flatulate
the minus 4 of power's ratios,
blow away at a breath of Bellini or Bach.
O hand sweet hand, thou intricate of the soul
through dances that might teach the heart its goal,
O able hand, what cut thee off at the wrist
to tell thee that all grace composed a fist?

GIORGIONE'S *TEMPEST*

It's fitting, on my forty-fifth
birthday, to celebrate a gift
from Giorgione, the sensualist
of joyous flesh, although a lost
synapse, a queer disrelation
dislocates accustomed emotion:
not only are foreground and background
at odds, but there's something crossgrained
betwixt the figures, almost a feel
of *waking or dream? of flesh or soul?*
Then why does it brood an ethical
continuity, until
it nearly engenders its opposite:
expectation? Separate,
the soldier prinks in a world he made;
but he might just as well be dead.
Not so the gypsy woman and child
(of a certainty no allegory
from Statius!). Giorgione's
lenient warmth melts over pearly
thigh and a breast's voluptuous
yet faultless activity and choice.
Between the woman and the soldier
distance lacks direction, is scalar
for all the full-blown grist of her flesh.
Their solitude of two discretes;
but it's landscape accommodates
the full *lontana* of emotion.
How can they, then, loiter so human,
as if their equivocation were all,
like ripeness, and the storm's pall

not at their frail backs? Torn brinks of cloud
riddle the storm's portent upward,
while backward it is blatantly charged
with disrelation's illumination
as the greenblue atmosphere, wind-urged,
goes lurid. . .   As if the lightning were not
burning estranged on that one white wall,
the luminous ultimate value of white,
a ghost afire? All that's asunder,
all disrelation, points to the long-sought
evading relation we'd all thought
to hide, the deft occlusion of thunder
confirmed in iridescent flesh.
All possible boil up at the flash
to include the painter, this spirit in league
with sense. No wonder the sky's perturbed
by itself in the pool! He, too, absorbed
his vision, who died at thirty-three
dissolved in the rosy flesh of plague.

PROSE FOR THE CHILDREN OF ABORTED REVOLUTION

In the *Las Meninas* of Velázquez, subjects are not the subject, neither is it the artist expressing or representing what he has chosen to paint. The whole of it is outside the picture, increasing the potential for moving inside. Otherlings — Infanta, courtiers, maids, even magnificent mastiff and complacently monstrous dwarf (who might have raped Snow White) — are unexceptionably objects whose mode of being revealed in space is composed by the presence of the royal couple situated outside and in front of the canvas, a presence that is in turn absent except as immersed in a mirror in the depths. Also in the depths, a figure who is possibly the painter's brother postures in a doorway, his gentlemanly presence seized in the very act of transforming itself into absence, a felt deficiency, equivocal, a verge like the disappearance of events into history and, beyond the door, beyond the mirror, the vanishing of history into epiphany. Indeed, there is a shadow beginning to lower over the glory of Spain. Sense it in the paint, a flickering of texture. Out of this shadow Velázquez the man shines like a new sun.

What terror is presented when a metaphysician disappears into a mirror, what panic when a public functionary, whether clerk in the Office of Records or President of the Republic, disappears into his majority, what blank misgivings when a poet disappears into prose!

Things, outclassed, narrow down and disappear. This painting is traveling through a tunnel at the speed of light. The light emanates from Velázquez.

THE GRATE
(looking at a painting by Gabriel Seidler)

for Susan

I knew I looked into the blazing throne
from whence all power derives and whither returns
all domination that Heraclitus had known,
where thought together with its shadow burns
on meteoric canvas, and in an eye —
this I thought, my glory-shout gone dumb
at so much pentecost and nascent cry.
Was I impatient for joy? Or had it come?
In darkness beyond, oracularly withdrawn
from fire, I muddled water with trees, two-edged
sweetflag leaves with one mad, hardly fledged
burst from a loon reverberant till dawn.
As if that fire were water, I was drunk
and stumbling on seed discharged from anthracite:
here trammeled lightning, wolf's gold, sunburst monk,
dragon's breath, St. Elmo, St. John's night
bonfires from hill to hill as if on wings
to show all scintillations one refined,
to bring in dawn when, as it must, dawn springs,
kindled shekinah in a painter's mind.
And unto Whom is drunken speech preferred?
As One should say: the mouth shall bear a sun,
Chrysostom through an incandescent word
though skull impersonate whole skeleton.
In time: wheels-within-wheels become a grate,
a grill, the pivot where I contemplate
that which with dragging belly, that which with wings
intersect and touch off vision, bestir
one hearth, O aerolite, O messenger
centered on the radiant surface of things!

75

MODEL FOR AN OBJECT IN X SPACE

It should have all the speed, tenacity
of waywardness, and tensile strength of a spring
decompressed against a neutral background,
this object (pried from the scrapped machinery
of mental habit) which, while rallying
experience, I pose as willfully sound.

I'd sooner, less discrepant, pose a nude:
voraciously pink, most Maja, she reclines
on a creamy, dwindling davenport — too snug
to hold her, so she coils up like a spring
prepared to strike
though in repose.
She snares blue shadows where her hollows beg
a fountain of strokes, caresses, palette-knife jabs,
hollows hungry for light, but negative.

A spring, unused, will rust to boredom. See,
the evenhanded background takes her red,
or hue of red, for granted, yet reacts
to the leap implied in depth as though a bee
had stung it. Whether coiled or sprung abed,
take care: she'll go berserk while pink impacts.

MODEL FOR AN OBJECT IN Y SPACE

It should have all the repose, fixedness
of tension, and intent of a spiral stair
compressed between two prongs of a seething station,
this object (pried quiescent from the stress
of mental presence) which, while poised to snare
experience, I pose as sound relation.

I'd sooner, less redundant, pose a nude:
carnal as Rubens, beauty has fallen asleep
on a creamy flux of davenport — too quick
to stay her, so she touches either end,
a fierce conductor
in her repose.
She snares blue shadows where her hollows beg
a fountain of strokes, caresses, palette-knife jabs,
hollows stable with light, but positive.

A stair, unused, will creak and buckle. See,
the seething station is corruptive, mind
implores absence, trains wear out their tracks.
Whoever saw such universality
return to junk and thrive? Racked in the bind,
she goes inert when background furor slacks.

MODEL FOR AN OBJECT IN Z SPACE

She must have all the flux and plenitude
of being now what she will be tomorrow
in metamorphosis against her ground,
this woman (pried from the oracular nude
of mental transition) whom, because I borrow
experience, I pose as urgently sound.

I'd sooner pose a spring or spiral stair
than fix in fine these pinks with penury
or snare ripe shadows in a stagnant pool.
As for her background, any old bed or chair
will serve the urgencies of how to be
at rest in motion, brooding the molecule.

A nude, misused, will function as caprice.
Seldom permit her cotquean counterpart,
likewise naked as hope or despair, to intrude,
for she'll not change position nor release
the infinite hams and eternal hocks of art
to model on the flux of plenitude.

VERSES AFTER WHICH THE MOURNING STATUE IS PRESUMED TO SPEAK

How speak to stone when stone and grief are mute to me?
    Though shaped by man, and both accused by time,
though dwelled in and suffered on Goliath forehead, stone
      is inexhaustibly that other world
where space, compressed, will let no angel in or out,
    but locks its head into its grieving arms.
No more than shape of body underneath her robes
      hunches on the marble sarcophagus
(plangent with the settling levitation of dust
      shriving with lime). The inscription's turned to her
("I shall go to him, but he shall not return to me")
    and away from us. If only she'd unlock
her arms, rigid with hermiting the stored lament,
      her deepest black of death would lighten life.
The sculptor lightened joy by an innocent deceit;
    for look: to read it we must turn our steps
to behind the statue, glorying over the grainy stone
      with hands that grow to love it, thumbs and all.

Though you, once woman, pass from mourning into myth,
      forgive us this, forgive us our joy in life,
      as we forgive ourselves for going to you.

HOUYHNHNM'S HOLIDAY

In white plaster, a neighing fellow
pillaged from the device of Uccello,
he champs, prances, decidedly
      male, and alone

— seeming life-sized in the foyer
where showy square teeth waylay
coatrack, rug, and taunt the settee —
      ce cheval blanc.

Into flung-back nostrils he's white
(except for glass eyes, black, and a night
of horsehair, coarse to its actual flea,
      pending behind),

to chalky straps and saddle, reins
and harness, that once on hurricanes
of azurine and cramoisy
      careened around.

You'd measure forty inches from
plump rump to where merged powers come
to each gracefully tucked front knee,
      some thirty two

from hooves planted at the rear
obliquely to the tip of an ear.
It lends uneasy symmetry.
      A metal rod

is perpendicular to sustain
him, thorax and neck, into his brain.
It's sure a comical sight to see
      this toy courser

discharging a whinny's merry round
though never uttering a sound.

Somewhere in the south of France
a merry-go-round that doesn't dance
misses, recurrently, a beat,
      unlike the world

its manifold. Around and around,
gap-horsed, while battered humstrums pound
and children assert discomfited seat
      on elephants,

gazelles, giraffes, on other horses,
the ratchety engine pursues its courses.
Indeed, this citadel's a cheat,
      a door warped

between arrival and departure,
sure not open, not closed to the marcher
intent on forgetting two left feet.
      Here's the journey

that never having known a goal
is doubly possessed by absence, the whole
estranging the part, incomplete.
      The evening star

is dangling from the ferris wheel.
Children wonder if they feel.

Nor parlays better in furniture's tongue,
this centaur's better half; too young
to prove our pact with nothingness,
        he duplicates:

"I am becoming a god, I think . . . "
But where's the pageant that made us blink,
barbaric reds, a blatant yes
        of gilt and orange

whirled in the furious blue, the south?
Green persimmon would sweeten his mouth.
As in his traveling days, duress
        of a child's weight

inhibits the hope of a caracole.
So unfelt pressures take their toll:
objective mill, belongingness,
        abstracted, disused;

the steady-seatedness of things
detached from boons and doles and stings,
function's circle squared, acquiesce
        in use abstracted;

as who should turn a transept back
into its idea's maniac
or architect's head — a sphere or less.
        But into whose

executive will could we reverse
this gift horse, placating its curse,
since even the curse is an excess
        of nothing to love?

Where plaster disappears I know
but where do merry-go-rounds go?

EXTRA-TERRESTRIAL FUNCTION OF SPOKES

While keeping circumference
from riding up on hub,
intermittent silence
rouses Beelzebub
from reveries of clatter.

Past the wheelwright bred
to *ah* and to *alas*,
iron-ribbed, tin-hearted,
tongue of sounding brass,
it makes wayfarers scatter

and glimpse while on the run
how night revolves with day
in rigor of division,
how vacancies convey
passage implicit with matter,

pursues them to the west
from wax to certain wane,
stalks them round from nearest
forfeit to farthest gain,
by fits and starts to batter,

until in the gloomy garage
it stops (is stopped to chance
no tranquil roots, no marriage
of failure and puissance)
and hub and rim shatter.

"I'D UNDERSTAND YER POEMES BETTER," WRITES THE LADY EDITOR FROM SAN FRANCISCO, "IF I KNOWED WHAT THE WORDS MEAN."

Abature: I think you'd all be better off
knowing the word: the traces that a stag
leaves in his flight through underbrush: the hunks
of fur on thorns, droppings when scared shitless,
that tang of musk behind him on the trail.
I've also left my furfur here and there:
dandruff in many a bed, a swollen sewer,
bellybutton lint on a pure high peak.
I think that we should stretch our vocabularies
just a smidgeon to keep dear English pure.

HARD FACTS

A close-mouthed lexicon of facts
secretes me in its middling acts;
ostents, modest at the start,
flourish, eating out my heart,
a heart not saintly to begin with,
barely beating enough to sin with.
O blood unable, sooner the moon,
to brood a sea or read a rune,
don't ask what you are tided to ask:
why, ebbed from memory, I task
arriving day with reverence
to meet my moments with its sense.
Be tender, too, buoyant with tact,
for dawn can be as hard as fact.
Facts would be unliveable
were they not unforgivable.

HENRY HUDSON

Sometimes we rearticulate history
to suit our human factor, not the facts:
thus when Hudson points the Half-Moon north
we're there! it's night! the fog's one seamless fleece!
He sails upriver and clean out of our world!

We all of us have our Northwest Passages,
our real estate explores heaven and hell.
Water's our body: we travel where we will.
He fills his canvas up an unnamed river,
becoming pure event, a fact, a name.

KOAN FOR TWO MINUTES OF
INTENSIVE MEDITATION

By means of metaphor
I learned that fruit is fruit
and flower flower, and more
when tuned on a poet's lute.
After instruction in Zen
fruit and flower were not-
fruit, not-flower. That's when
sole speech turned polyglot.
I figured the matter moot
until I found through power
of revelation that fruit
is fruit and flower flower.

THE LOCK

Take heart! Your zebra will make
its personal jailbreak,
radiant in its bars
will leap the estranging wall,
eyes let down to stars
that lift it lightyears tall.
While it outstarts the fox
and curls the lion's locks,
while the turnkey's chain
rusts from its glowing brain,
under its hooves the fire
that gems the scum and mire
lights proud Empedocles
the way to find his knees.
Then your zebra returns
and in your freedom burns.

This was testified me
on my first poem's threshing floor,
when first I held a key
and knew it for no door.

SIGNING THE POEM

Echo in the mirror's not potential
and thus is dissidently possible.
Echo, contingent between two cliffs or mirrors,
unseen in either, "a night," as Hegel declares,
"in which all cows are black," the predicables
& other predicaments, is possible
and what may be indeed: the cry of mirrors
as they destroy our luck for seven years.
We wait a lifetime for the least event
to surface, then it's gone — first child, first book.
This line, soul-forged, mind-dazzled, fused to the page
(itself a mirror for the dwindling phrase),
already over, drags me, memory
and all I imply, from import, in language
impenetrable and lucid become itself.
That line set nowhere on the road to nowhere;
this line's an overpass above that road:
once passed, its memory's unspeakable,
but turns Chrysostom's learnèd mouth to gold.
Thus there's a word for every thought, and words
for that which stirs beyond our every thought
yet must return at last: bird-migrations;
that arm, our own, trembling in its reach:
this look of distance on the face of approach.

DEAR MR. WORLDLY WISEMAN

"My language is my world."
— Wittgenstein

Despoiled of speech, defended poorly by birds,
your brother returns, whose prodigality
restored strangers to their primordial words
but left him wasted as a winter's tree
and stammering a dispossession of surds.

He sought for hours before he found his home,
since there was nothing of all that love retrieves:
all razed, all subdivided, calf into chrome,
the garden gone that gossiped amongst its leaves,
the newborn dead in the plazas of chromosome,

mother dead and father walled up for mad,
the irreducible magma paved, and you,
in sole possession, mute, can only add
outrage to the origins whose dew
gives morning to his meanings good or bad.

But while the air is his — and it is! the air
which neither dies nor frenzies, a constellation
of manna, of silk, of rose, of bell aware
of silence — the ancestral imagination
will place its hidden word into his care;

and while the air is his he'll hear the sound,
maybe at first a whisper dissolved in tears
and fire, in water boiling for rice, in ground
broken for grain, become a roar in his ears,
the world's outlasting name, pristine, profound;

a word, hermetic, simple, pronounced to restore
the world to its son; maybe only an AND,
a process, an innumerable door,
that bridge. You cannot hope to understand.
He had not thought to spend or ask for more.

PRIMEVAL LANDSCAPE WITH POLITICIAN
AND DODO BIRD

That afternoon when Monsoor Mouse
merged with the universe at large,
he lumbered crashing through the swale
and roared across the plain. He choired,
"I am the prevalent green" and trees
went bouncing to the far and near;
"*La savane, c'est moi*" and the soil
transmitted passion to the worm.
How can the sun transform his world
with that tiny gray mouse on the loose?

IMPROMPTU WITH A BREEZE

Slyly diverted, a breeze passes
through the billowing open window
into my room. Now that outside
has finished pushing its floral and mulish rump,
the breeze stops plump upon the wall
to con the wallpaper, mouldy,
overflowered once, only once.
    If I open the door this breeze can give place to
fresh breezes. I'm not Pythagoras
by a nose. But also, if I do so,
two maudlins, that radio'd bitch next door
and a cuckold whose wife last week committed
rapture will, with their collective snout,
    root in the vegetable of this sheet
that began — O devoted irresolution —
with a breeze, a welcome breeze.
Hang those curtains and this address!
    Now look what this damned poem has got me into.
    What would Mr. Blackmur say to this?

POEM WRITTEN ON THE TYPEWRITER

Despoiled and machine-honed as I am, I guess
contraption should meddle between me and the page,
at least this once. What if the poem be less?
What matters is keeping in and up with the age.

I'm awkwardly ill-at-ease. I sense a presence,
deep-jowled but chapfallen, sneering behind me,
though panic rhymes pin down hysterical sense.
Among these clattering keys, kobolds find me.

Keys stick. Nothing works. Sparks click in the dark.
There's always been an It: it seems I'm it.
From what shall I compile my survival kit?
A madman's crawling from under the question mark.

EPISTLE TO SIMON PERCHIK

Yours received :those cursory notes
in your impatient, poky script
on margins of the poems you sent.
Yet Simon's hardly in the letter;
no apple cheeks, not much of the mind
that makes of him so prime a lawyer
and poet packed with concerned insight,
no dapper overcoat, no self-
deprecating grin, no fun.
But Simon's verse was in the letter;
or, more precisely, two versions
of one lyric, the later one
an apt and thoughtfully provided
homily on how to reduce
language to lowest denominator
and repel nuanced punctuation
in an addicted miscellany
of colons, tiered and permissive :not
with Dante's *amorosa lima*
but with a buzzsaw amputating
those delicate particles :oh, not
that all's not reaching out and moving
and even universal :though
I've never worn government issue,
all old garments absorb the affects
of uniforms when rediscovered
years after the pathos of routine.
Though beauty amid mayhem's granted,
the noble articles sustained
severe losses, and though their corpses

have been removed from the field, signs
of slaughter everywhere meet the ear.
Desertion of these helpful particles
is the symbolic relinquishment
— at least impoverishing — of choice,
and so much must not be conceded
the adversaries of simple needs,
whether survival's or poetry's.

Consider, a moment, those articles.
"Bring me the book," if not to bible,
refers to a determined book
about which writer and reader share
some tacit knowledge. Simon, how
priceless nowadays to share
even concern so small! Besides,
"the" isolates the substantive
from limitless vagueness of common nouns
and presents it as focus of intention.
Thus the article supposes
a reification of the essence
expressed by the noun alone, yet not
concretized like "there" or "that."
Further note that any word
or phrase or sometimes tome, preceded
by one of our articles becomes
a single noun, so arguing
the staggering possibility
of substantivizing the universe,
which is better than conquering her,
and attends to differences between.
And I've a hundred reasons more!
So don't relinquish your competence

in permeating life with choice,
friend Simon, lest (as once your namesake)
you leap from the tower of your poem
into a void of dire compulsion,
a Rome whose language comes to grief
from the barbarians within.

EPISTLE TO SUZANNE JOSLYN FOSBERG

"All Bedlam, or Parnassus, is let out."
—Alexander Pope

No day for work; a day to strut and ramp.
The sun has stuck its special-delivery stamp
on today's blue envelope. Noon's royal flush
scoops up its winnings midst a luminous hush.
Yet, by refuting your hypnoperboles,
Suzanne, I'll treat your luminous mind's disease.
Mark how they end, those nerves that squirm and twitch,
in tenements that make your body rich;
whatever's sought in them, their little good,
struggles stupidly to be understood,
and will be, if we have not failed belief
in what we are: the art so long, life brief.

The first among your lapses is to call
meter rhythm. Rhythm inheres in all
you speak and write, in painting, music, dance,
as prime in prose as in any utterance.
Distinguish that huge surge from meter; then,
and only then, pick up the critic's pen.
Rhythm engages reasonableness, and choice,
while meter corresponds to passion's voice:
in fury, triumph, dread, and ecstasy
our speech approaches regularity.
Our prosodists and linguists there agree.
Analysis eschews spellbinding norms,
but passion stamps its will on what it forms.
Meter's lagniappe, she's counter rhythm, counter-
point where news and implication mount her

to breed a subtle double, fixed, irregular,
a flower small enough to hold a star.
Do meters appall? That scarecrow's filled with birds.
Our metric sings not only through our words
but through the universe: the constellations
pursue the seasons, both configurations
in ample order, countable on your wrist:
through waves, through tides. A meteorologist
knows meter. Wedge your hand beneath your breast
to feel our verse and world unstressed and stressed.

The sunshine through my window slantwise slashed
keeps me adhesive to my desk. The cached
heat is accumulating in the sweat
that drips to ask me: must we acquit this debt?
We must, we will; it is our only bet.
Some nightmare strands you in a haunted mind —
hardly your own — the age's — where you find
disorder is the order of the day.
Mind's commode flushed, you hear hubbub betray
indigestion in the stark plumbing's guts.
Free verse, that's neither verse nor free, time's klutz,
is prose not only chopped but lopped of sense
except to such as muddles make pretense,
a donkey's compass of indignant song
for sensibility it senses wrong.
When will we learn a mere slick and a premise
is all that's left of wordless tune and promise?
And they're so dull! no shine, no razzle-dazzle
as mind and nerves are worn down to a frazzle.
And how they proliferate! Parnassus now
swarms with buffoons whose National Endow-
ment checks are more inventive than their odes.

Such windy verse, strummed on one chord, erodes
the poet where he lives — plantation of myth
and mansion of sound. And yet, confronted with
that great guerrilla chief of Twickenham,
homespun and scarlet take it on the lam
not to be stung by cinq-paced scorpions
expulsing them from pseudo-Helicons.
Ambrosia's washed from mouths by the soft soap
of every Prior claiming he is Pope.
And all for lack of meter. So, Suzanne,
nothing in verse does more than meter can
to set our rhythm free. Without the waves
riptide would have no force, and nothing saves
from winter like the prescience of spring.
Oh, it's a night for odes, for everything
as constant as Orion's hunt! The west
is darkly pregnant with tomorrow's best;
an owl has eaten the sun, but that's all right,
the moon is rising, metrical with light.

POET'S BESTIARY

Prologue

Beyond the symbol's exactions, we transform
our verse into those creatures we admire,
protesting: "Here am I! But only when warm
or jumpy . . . " admitting more than we'd desire,

or often into bestial forms we hate,
incorporating thus a sacrifice
we'd never offer but the aesthetic heat
incubates then prods the spirit's lice,

for all these moral beasts, make no mistake,
from Yeats' trimmers to Lawrence's elephants,
Catullus' envied sparrow to Moby Dick,
creep in tendoned metamorphosis.

Nor marvel, diligent reader, if at times
poets seem in the cages, squinting out
at vertebrates their phrase no longer tames:
many's the god by good works put to route.

The Tour

> [*Our curator, the genial Marianne Moore,*
> *who performs the duty of conducting this tour,*
> *cannot be with us. We don't know where she's at*
> *since she vanished into the smile of the Cheshire Cat.*]

Inside that tank the dread leviathan
that swallowed Jonah basks on ample back.
Echoic ages turned him pallid and thin
till he took nourishment from Melville's book,

102

whence scholars bagged him, brought him to ivied halls
(queer environment for such a fury!)
and in this colorful setting of pasteboard hulls
display him to a self-complacent jury.

In this dark cage the milkwhite unicorn
Sidonius dreamt encloses a sunny garden
where Mary stoops to pluck its festering thorn
with never a thought to free the captive warden.

There's the vacant roost whence Shakespeare's lark
took wing for regions shied from by the bard;
and Dryden's hind, wherein archbishops lurk,
and even moppets know the pulpit's bared.

Kit Smart was one whose vast menagerie
took to scratching and screeching in his brain,
forcing him out on the streets to kneel and pray,
leaping again to sing and praise and groan,

till pious powers locked him away in a cage
with clerical rats his merriest company;
then Jeoffry arrived, purring so gentle a purge
he gave the vermin a chance to steal away.

Blake's tyger stood too long in lightning weather,
Blake's wild mind (without that prissy lamb)
forged in a fire, romping on any tether,
springing from the poem's exalted limb

on heads of unsuspecting innocence,
clawing his way inside. In rapt surmise
he's hunched, devouring with the reader's sense,
Blake's eyes glaring out of his victim's eyes.

Though Baudelaire turned sacrificial words
into a foolish, castrate albatross,
he wouldn't disavow the death-to-birds
that through his loins purred to his distress,

for look! a wind that weeps through nothingness
has knocked him off his feet, and, flat on his back,
he artifices a sanctum of tinsel, glass,
abolishing spontaneous bird and cat.

His stout friend, Gautier, an arty tidbit,
brooded over a hippopotamus
(the same that Eliot so archly sat)
and how it pound by pound adopted his muse.

Cowper's neat antithesis to Thoreau
would shore one hare against the state of fear
that risked his garden, England. He would grow
mad antlers in the dark, a "stricken deer."

A wolf, that most remote, most haughty thane,
was De Vigny's ideal of a bond:
tonight a wolf still solos to the moon
while stars, still heeding, still refuse to bend.

Than ravens galled Villon found little worse,
lamped dead eyes frothed up as by detergent;
but to Leconte de Lisle they were his muse,
spectator of world-madness, and its agent;

yet he, aspiring to Plato in the flesh
of Aphrodyte, couldn't conclude a meal
he dreamt of at the foot of Holy Cross
of which a raven had foretold each nail.

Afraid he'd disappear, lacking his mirror,
Mallarmé imprisoned his swan's white wing
in a clear mirror of ice, proving in terror
that even out of nothing he could sing.

By his hyena-self Rimbaud was cornered
and laughed until he ached: he'd done 'em brown!
But *schadenfreude*, stench of all he'd bartered,
was chief of boons to hunters tracking him down.

Small toads would serve self-blackwashed, vain Laforgue's
ironic ego. Social swamps take flight.
So cherished the moon, mother to filigreed morgues,
since toads (like moons) are citizens of night.

Gloomier Hardy with his darkling thrush
connived at a spellbound condominium:
what the bird knew would make the poet blush,
what the bard knew would make the warbler dumb.

Gentle Jammes, than Shakespeare more courageous,
ambled heavenward and took an ass.
Such comradeship to wisdom's advantageous:
where flawed sainthood might not, patience would pass.

A pink flamingo in a castle pond
whispered Rilke secrets intended to maim,
panther's stride repeated the close-lipped wound,
but only a rose would speak death's idiom.

Jeffers gave a woman a stallion to love,
but for himself reserved uncaring hawks.
When not a rock, his heart became a dove
exposed, like trulls, where mutilation lurks.

A snake turned Lawrence invertebrate
in imitation of that slithering god,
magical expiation of a guilt
not petty, yet pious, joyful under the rod.

Lorca's black bull, endemic to his race,
a burgeoning in the state of constant things,
from man to man is sung, to each his cade,
from each his life suspended in a ring,

abevacuation of desire
that murdered Lorca in Machado's blood
and drowns Alberti's pride in Mithra's mire.
Did Noah build for this against the flood?

Epilogue

An arbitrary closure is implied
by countless sand on only seven seas,
as by those chains of logic which would plead
forever. "Break them!" advised Parmenides.

ANACREONTIC FOR A CHINESE SCHOLAR

When not disintricating the Yi Ching's knots
you hunch in your comfortless cell, meticulous,
and English the tart drunken odes of Li Po
(who died embracing the moon in a giddy river)
or Tu Fu (who absorbed the shocks of war
by hallowing the pot with friends). Dear friend,
many-allonymèd Bacchus weeps
in his cups for you. You know how salt spoils wine?
Well, tremble; for while you meditate the Change
& Process, Bacchus reels in, stoned to the eyes,
to belch by your sober bench, and dangles you
between two fingers like a yarrow stalk.

107

NIGHTMARE SONG

A boy, I played agile and difficult games
compounding daring with skill under that bridge,
fine weather and foul drawn
by shelter, structure, the big blue drops of sky,
while pigeon shadows swooped and the river ran
on & on.

Well, Mr. Berryman, if character
be destiny, your poems must have wept
as you and the bridge converged
and Hardy leaned sighing from his cloud.
You only saw dismayed how dreams became
your demiurge.

So steel and concrete flourish in my head,
new leaves tightening their hold like bolts,
running hard roots for rain,
girders gossiping in the dark when John
drags Henry under and does in Mister Bones
again & again.

SCENE FROM LIFE

Out of a distant past this tableau sticks:
my father, one foot up on a runningboard, flicks
     his Old Gold butt and passes the hooch, a girl
is reading Hergesheimer, one determined curl
     glued to her forehead, a fuller woman, young
and blonde, makes goo-goo eyes at father, mother's tongue
     explores her lip, she wipes her hands, the cat
slips out of the children's reach, the loveable family dingbat,
     Uncle Bert, shoots tincans out of the air,
I cannot see myself but I am certainly there,
     the last guest at table, watching steam
lifting from vegetable soup in an unwavering stream.
     These are not totems memory would choose,
but work of scummy nostalgia, brother-in-law to booze.

POEM TO BE PRINTED ON A VERY WHITE PAGE

"No confidence in dis poor ole darkie, den?"
— Melville

Trust at least in this bird
caroling from the top branch
of ecstasy, whose song
devours its shadow with flame.
When I declare its word
consumes it, feathers and name,
I do not mean to wrong
its meaning in disguise
of phoenix, quetzal, crow,
nor fretfully demand
a syntax for its cries.
Simply I need insist
that here's the age's harvest
of ashes held in the hand
of God. Open your fist!
This song has won its right
to silence. Trust to its light.

BARRIER SNOW

"The time of premonition is thought."
— Laura Riding

The world ends at the barriers of snow.
    Where edges are solid the winds sing;
     sun looks in, but does not glow.
Retreat: not many penetrate this ring.
       To and fro,

through wheels of blizzard, three thin sycamores
    try shivering back into the world
    proscribed them by the cold's white spores
each round an imp of dust in crystals curled,
      insistent cores

in chaos where a cardinal broke through
    to flutter south, benumbed but free.
    Queen Anne's lace and feverfew,
whipped against the flurried masonry,
      rattle askew.

Crystalizing in the eye's fixed yield,
    attention's instant of blinking shifts,
    returns, while mind and its own, congealed
on perception, sink. Small wonder that the drifts
     submerge the field.

Barriers trespassed by the farther unseen
    conduce to where the mind in its flake
    evolves the possible of green.
The wonder is the body will not wake
    to intervene.

LOGOS

While wordlessly admiring an ancient wall,
  it's cracked and porous net of texture
    where nothing's accidental,

not even faint blue, lemon and pale rose
  irised to a shimmer under
    pellucidly white surface,

I sighted a lizard there who chose to cling
  exactly in the betraying center,
    immobile as not-being,

a lizard whose consciousness, in quid pro quo,
  became a fly or, far from terror,
    the cold rim of my shadow,

a lizard like dusty salvias, dead man's skin
  left to shrivel as a reminder
    that purpose won't be hidden,

until in the light's crackle and cauldron roar
  pulsing was suddenly salamander
    and I could see it no more.

ANONYMOUS SECRETS

Simply by opening these eyes
the world is made. You may visit
there but not on our lives inhabit
       my reticences.
I've got to be prudent what I view,
double the stakes, for our protection
be motion, tact, be circumspect
       in theory, echo.
Any distraction from what is,
a blink, unmakes this complete world:
your eye from function's disenthralled,
       shells forget seas.
Just watch me make your visit welcome!
But since I'm blind you're on your own.
White ink on a white page. No one
       knows who I am.

FROM WHEREVER I AM

Devotion, I had thought, to my vocation
was all my arrears, until I stumbled onto
the millstone, earnest of my civilization,
milestone midway between volcano and statue,
and had to grind to capture the crowd's ovation.

Those indestructible birds that die in song-stress,
yet sing to us still, live in the marble moment
that shivers under the mallet's pounce. Their progress,
formal as matter, marks the silent torrent
and shatters the heart of any lesser songstress.

Volcanic ash and quarry are forsaking
Aphrodyte toppled into a midden,
a bone structure at odds with its mask, meekmaking,
caryatid with torso demolished by cannon.
The mansion's vandalized: teak for the taking.

My epitaph's a too short epigram:
He ground his touchstone thin. Although unskilled
at pleasing the crowd, I've bowed and welcomed sham.
Oh, I'm so cold, cold from within, so cold
from wherever I am not whatever I am.

SILENUS' EPITAPH

for Jack McManus

So now I keep my caution company.
All a day I capered astride a wineskin,
but at long last drowsed, and thereon slept,
on either side a satyr keeping watch,
horrid against rogue-errant's coming with garlic
chains to indenture me to prophecy.
    They tippled; I was caught and forced
    to tattle: tongue tripped lightly, sun
    and wine well met, but caution dead.
So now I keep my caution company. . .
    Tread softly. Huger than my hot head
    there's nothing, nor smaller than my sense.
Imminent as forever, my utterance
freezes to the lips of eternity
who smiles, and laughs to keep me company.

IV

HAND

This is my dream. And always again
its secret pries my eyes apart
without restoring me awake.

The withered hand of the croupier
grips mine in sly complicity,
then hale and strong gets back to work.
Outside the casino, down a dark
street, I stroll with Randall Jarrell.
We mull things over, notice the thugs
who stalk us, slinking like C.I.A.,
but can't afford to pay them mind.
At 3 a.m. they strike. They smash
our Randall. "This is for Procter!" one screams.
Another to me: "And that for Gamble!"
Awake, I cannot grip my pen
for hours, for days, for centuries.
My hand is dropping off on my desk
and in revenge — revenge on whom? —
inscribes the word that ends all books
and never quite became a word.

SHAKESPEARE IN VIETNAM

WESTMORELAND: O that we now had here
But one ten thousand of those men in England
That do no work today.

HENRY V: . . . . . No, my fair cousin:
If we are marked to die, we are enow
To do our country loss; and if to live,
The fewer men, the greater share of honor.

A later man, one of the amorphous
Johnson clan, a folksy, oily tyrant,
found that honor crossed with money well,
and blood on both, as long as not his own,
could bring a mule of life into his eyes.
Those who refuse his bloody work today
cry shame and call for fair impeachment. One
cannot divide his honor into two
and grow: such profit is his country's loss,
while Henry's ultimate was to fight alone.
As for Westmoreland, always attrition's fool,
he brays because his master's now his tool.

CERTAIN PARALIPOMENA TO AN UNBEGUN EPIC

I met a master of demolition
    conspiring with his beer.
A garrulous man and a dyspeptic,
    he stated, "Sometimes I fear
all hero's courage is a shibboleth
    and salivates the fine intentions
        that make the state cohere."
The hero, we owe him life, we owe him death.

I met a rugged base commander,
    vulgar, his face beet-red,
a lion invariably triumphant,
    although he's never bled.
All hero's courage is a shibboleth.
    That he's too scared to bugger his brother
        has never entered his head.
The hero, we owe him life, we owe him death.

I met Lieutenant Calley, befuddled
    on piss and vinegar.
He told me how for my sins he suffers
    and pointed to every scar.
All hero's courage is a shibboleth.
    I learned the workings of the nation
        when he sprang for my jugular.
The hero, we owe him life, we owe him death.

I met a hero of the market,
   an individualist,
who poked his face in mine and shouted,
   "My winds blow whither I list!"
(All hero's courage is a shibboleth.)
   He's thrown up by the mass's boiling;
      once gone, he is not missed.
The hero, we owe him life, we owe him death.

I met a victim whose tour of duty
   first fattened, then ate his youth.
He preached a new crusade for children
   and flashed a golden tooth.
All hero's courage is a shibboleth.
   A hero may call all heroes liars,
      a liar for telling the truth.
The hero, we owe him life, we owe him death.

IMITATION OF HORACE
Carmina, I.6

No, I'll not do it, I'll not! Conscript
some bard of epic splendor and scope,
some Capote lisping grandly in numbers;
some Winchell or Schlesinger with a harp
shall your praises hymn, I'll not; nor laud
your hireling who, with capsuled germ concealed
in green beret, and under your command (O Caesar
first to storm the nation's whistlestops)
lays low the Asian village. Oh, how I fear
the atom up his sleeve
might scorch his wrist!
I dread the swarm and push; and fear my verse,
however free, might not permit of being trained
to take the liberties you push to take.
I can lead my Pegasus to that Helicon
but damned if I can get him to drink!
Instead, give me my genius' optimum use.
I'd sing the metaphysic subtleties
of mirror, guilt, the thought behind the thought.
If combat you must have, I'd sing
the combat of randy hand and silky thigh.
I'd compliment my host on his choice of wines
and rubricate my choice of friends on the calendar.
I'll praise the Negro that he snaps his chains
(now neatly relinking in the name of Vietnam)
and the three pink streaks that make a white carnation
what in truth it is. And once again
those randy hands and silky inner thighs
from which all good and evil generate.

A FORM OF PITY

Posture of an innocence presumes
climate where the passions effloresce
in strangling vines and strange carnivorous blooms,
such beauties as the heart cannot profess
despite the roses filling up our rooms.
Damned be pity when it's pitiless!

TRAJECTORY OF A SCREAM

For, suckling her baby and glimpsing on the wall
a glare that from some hundreds of miles away
exploded to warn her still another day
was devastated past the age's recall,
how could she know her lyric milk, turned gall,
would work in the child till he outshrieked the jay?
Whatever she knew, the woman would never say,
but drew her icy sheet tight in a pall
and pulled down the ceiling roaring round her head.
The horror survived, the horror survived and grew
some years before we started wishing it dead.
The final sign was: both eyes fused to one,
dilating as wreckage clotted its smoky flue,
then, with implosions, burnt out like a sun.

ELEMENTAL TRUST

Fission has turned our barracks ghostly.
The possibility of rhomboids, wheels
and troglodytes has been removed, also
of painted caves
and hymns that arched our barbarous heads with naves.
Only the creatures remain —
outsized roaches and rats, mostly.

Rats are running through forest and field
and rubble of towns, comely as on the day
of their creation. Dew along their backs
is crystal. Perhaps
they see the world they shared before the lapse.
Me they seem not to see.
Even their sore of hunger is healed.

Fur clean, eyes full and clear, they speak
to me, lone human survivor, an idiom
less grisly than my father's. In their reserves
of avatar,
their uncorrupted innocence, they are
the promise of purer life.
I'll try their teeth along my cheek!

THE PINCH

The pinch lies in the shoe of state;
pride has toe'd us to this pass;
a limping soul has made us late.

What on our backs is pending freight
was lighter than a waltz on grass:
the pinch lies in the shoe of state.

Self-righteously, we exculpate
our dividends in Childermass.
A limping soul has made us late

while reconciling to that fate.
It doesn't help to step on the gas.
The pinch lies in the shoe of state.

Ask those ahead if they will wait,
for we have somewhere lost our ass;
a limping soul has made us late.

It's not fear's pebbles preponderate;
the road, though hard, is clear as glass.
The pinch lies. In the shoe of state,
a limping soul has made us late.

MOTIVES OF A TWO-HEADED TURTLE

No moral doctor could more nicely pose
the problem of how far and how well free.
Far from respite, even in submerged dreams,
down two dusty roads at once he goes,
a workshop in the directions of direction,
but soon must halt for bearings, not to be forked,
not to be stretched on something not his sort
of dust or mud. Like ours, his predilection
drums its own beat; though he, alas, has two
for every want. He snaps up twice the gnats,
keeps well informed where dearest foe is at,
can duck both noggins at once — that much is true.
It gets him, if not nowhere, surely not far:
all his commission, spread-turtled on the proof
of binary volition, needs must endure
his unco-ordinates, not that canard
of Zeno's. A species (turtle, say, man or bee)
"through individuals realizing itself"
can never elucidate self-consciousness,
for choice is teleologically free
or else the turtle would be wholly his past.
Only a self can undertake to turn
desires into motives. Meanwhile, as with Church
and State, a parting of ways helps to contrast
a choosy if turgid libertarian stance,
rich in alternatives, with room for caprice,
and blank determination's bubble and squeak,
where even one head's victimized by chance.
A will which, though not much, was to its creature
nonesuch, enough, and absolute puissance,
not competition subdividing its chance,

is now stopped vulnerable in the road. His teacher,
Anima Mundi, licks him up with the dust
and spits him out in more ways than he cares
to push primordial luck. While most will bear
freedom, few are disposed by deed to trust
the choice; yet freedom from these plates, custod-
ial inversion of wings, will finicky rear
its ugly heads if he decides to learn
the shellback nature of the indifferent road.
When Aunt Mary Moody Emerson
rode through the streets of Concord in her shroud,
her motive was to keep from shrieking aloud.
The turtle merely wants to choose as one.

INTERPRETATION OF HIGH FINANCE

Able, just, or maybe not quite so,
    maybe not quite able yet,
        to know
the justice of possession without the binding debt.

The debt itself must put possession in doubt:
    maybe not quite ever able
        to flout
a finder's person for the keeper's nine-point fable.

St. Thomas found how debts confront the just
    possession of even a heavenly home,
        how trust,
once it probes wounds, can engineer no honeycomb.

And so to Parthia to proselytize.
    His manna
    (operative in poverty's guise)
should have held vital forces together in one hosanna,

at least his bethel in the midst of a wood
    that stands
    amidst a desert that's withstood
prosperity since rock first wore to doubtful sands.

Two lovers, faithfully breaking his bread, are sym-
    pathet-
    ic to possessions stored by him
in his heaven, or wherever, but are not able quite yet

to credit the subliming of excrement,
　　　　　　　the spout-
　　　　ing cornucopias that vent
shimmering gold walls whose doorways enter in and out.

　　　　But Thomas dies. The woods revert
　　　　　　　to waste.
In opposite directions, the lovers desert
the body unburied where it fell, maybe ungraced,

　　　　and leave their tracks in trackless sands,
　　　　　　　as deep
　　　　and unpossessable as fire-brands
at dead of night. The binding debt is never cheap.

The justice of possession affords no cost
　　　　　　to match the doubt's final request
　　　　　　　for the lost:
by his possessions the possessor is possessed.

NIGHT CRAWLERS

"People who work for me don't smoke."

"We'll likely go back to San Francisco . . . "

"People who work for me don't drink wine."

"Likely we won't work for you."

"People who work for me only eat vegetables."

"Fuck you and your piano!"

"Anyhow, come on down for a mess of greens."

Hunger casts out anger.

Except for hunger, nothing, not even the future of a
thunderclap's aftershine, is darker than Big Sur midnight.

Our host admonished us to take care crossing the bridge,
no more than two trunks over the below, unfathomable perhaps,
who-knows-how-deep-to rocks craving our transfixable glory?
Oh, how we bellyinched across, splinters demanding and getting
blood, rotgut gurgling loud as sluiced water, cry of coyote,
bat of owl's eye, width itself abyssal in this dark gut.

"Birds that fly on the map are not my birds," said our
host, chuckling from the gained side.

Next morning two trunks three feet above the babbling
creek were spread before our eyes.

If God's 99th name is "Bridge In Darkness," what is the
hundredth? Or do we start all over again?

NATIONAL ANTHEM
(Imitation of Carlos Drummond de Andrade's "*Hino Nacional*")

We need to discover America.
Hidden behind its factories and installations,
among its rivers, mountains, woods,
a just America lies asleep.
We need to colonize America.

We need to educate America.
If you need a president, why not black or red?
Every American must have a home
and in it music to weather timber and stone,
the pictures and books that bring life to life,
around it solar power, flowing water, soil.
We need to liberate America.

We need to praise America.
No country can equal us,
not even ourselves. Our revolutions
are bigger and better, also our mistakes.
And what of virtues? A land of sweet reason
and unreasonable passions, incredible John Does.

We need to love America.
No matter how hard to fit so much ocean and loneliness
into a heart already overcompromised,
no matter how hard to grasp what it is these men want,
no matter why they congregate in cities and agonize.

Above all what we need is to forget America.
So majestic, so illimitable, so unintentional!
It wants a respite from our terrible embraces.
America doesn't want us. It is fed up to here!
America's another world. This isn't a shining majesty.
There's no America — only, maybe, Americans.

A MONKEY'S ADDRESS TO OTHERS OF HIS KIND

Who can doubt that all the world's a zoo
with panthers, unicorns, us, and a few rare men
the only creatures to whom credit's due.
Yes, I'll declare it now who said it when
the last of the above-named whims was new
and innocent of Zen.

Out of our store of cunning we caused cages,
so disposing that their tenants think
themselves outside and peering in. Ambages
captivate them, ad hominem: they wink
at us while they're examined by our sages.
Peanuts are their egregious kink.

Love panthers for sweetness, for courage. There they shine,
eclipsing men and even unicorns.
Less redhanded than men, they've got more spine
and never trumpet their fame on counterfeit horns.
So love them for their allspice breath. Men dine
on cheer that would sour acorns.

Now unicorns are wondrously like goats,
yet more adept, and with dizzy "anfractuous spires."
But so perverse is man his anecdotes
delineate these virgin-hunting livewires
as eunuchs overawed by petticoats.
Observe how all conspires

to make of man a knave or else a fool.
His discourse 'd make your tail uncurl forever!
"Keep it frantic," he hollers, "like keep it cool!"
While lacking our wisdom, he is not unclever,
extracting stupendous purses from misrule.
Mon semblables, trust one never.

Although destructive without our joy in the acts
as pure noumina, he seems not unawares
of grace. Where he breaks down is over facts —
apples, beauty, atoms — all scaly with snares.
I wouldn't suggest you love what scarcely attracts,
yet in prayers, remember your forebears.

EPISTLE TO SPENCER HOLST

"Our distant Int'rests, and our different Passions
Now haste to mingle in one common Center,
And Fate lies crouded in a narrow space."
— Irene: III. vi. 3-5

So Doctor Johnson. Now it serves my pleasure
to wrench one blank into heroik measure,
for Sam's are flat, and I'll dare criticize:
Yet in that narrow Space what Dangers rise?
I'd bank that in the crowd of those five feet
Danger's averted, measure made discreet,
and, as verse goes, it proved no chore.
Damned if I haven't just committed one of four!
Danger on all sides menaces our skill:
if Hubris doesn't squelch us, Humble will.
Our peril, Spencer, lurks at those extremes;
but in between them all's not as it seems.
Shun parks by day, fountains at noon; beware
the mugger at the turning of the stair;
police locks bolt you in, not burglar out.
So how can you escape? It's mayhem to doubt
a sports car's ambush round each bend, or worse,
an instant's blink and presto! it's a hearse.
Going out for *The Times,* panics grow
sour stomach-balls. So where are you to go?
Cancer's snug in peanuts, ulcer in spice;
that Common Center could but won't entice:
a prothalamium is on the prowl
to score a tuneful marriage, cheek by jowl
with her those recreational engineers
in hotpink stretchpants answer to hate's leers
by making whoopee with our mights. There's more

than hue and clinkers in the wind. No floor
beneath you, overhead no ceiling. The true
poser to solve is: What are you to do?
As once Paul Goodman taught us, disappear
when THEY approach you, never volunteer.
To save your skin it's most expedient
to seem, though not to be, obedient.
Speak well of Manson's Mom, of Nixon's Dad,
extol the kiddies though they drive you mad.
Relinquish, post by post, positions of power,
or avalanche a thousand in an hour,
and then, from shrubbery, cellars, caves, fight back
so subtly they won't grasp you've got the knack.
Disguise and flight are not the worst of games.
An accident conceals designs and aims,
in service of which fact Polonius died.
But, Spencer, ready a safer place to hide.
Get from behind the arras, grab your chance
while your particular hangman's at a dance.
Then, too, a little honest hocus-pocus
(something like turning safflower into crocus)
stops them from framing your motives in their focus.

Once upon a time the suavest jackal
that ever raised a stink or vulture's hackle,
engaged an annointed lion in debate
above their prone gazelle, before they ate.
The jackal, versed in chopping logic, paced
a very lawyer, earnest-eyed, two-faced:
"Since seldom do we chumble living flesh,
be sure that savants would not have it fresh;
for Death proceeds, and thus the longer dead
the deader; ergo, black meat's better than red."
Against which case the lion advanced his own:

137

"The speciousness of your deduction's shown
by sciolism in your argument;
for Death is retrogressive, not procedent,
and retro-Satan halts at childhood's norms;
ergo, the younger the kill the more it warms
heart's cockles, and besides . . . " But here gazelle,
gripping her life, evading the citadel
of death unsound and logic bogus, rose
and tiptoed off, though sadly comatose.

Not the preposterous lion, Spencer, not
that grosser beast, the jackal, nor the rot
they tear between them, but the gazelle, her grace,
the flit, skedaddle, triumph in the race
I sing. That shoestring I would have you lace.
I maunder. So much confidence abuses
our finally acataleptic muses.
Let the hunters argue ways and means.
Remove your priceless hide from dangerous scenes,
a king who sheds his purples for blue jeans.

J'

for Lee Stothers

I've launched my inkpots at the fiend, but he
torpedoes them right back at me, no prophecies
but Rorschachs till the wall is drowned.
And so it is I've come to pray:

Take him to thee, Lord of little kittens;
let this bundle of tortoise fur be air, be soil,
to mouse, to hound. He hadn't even a name.
He knew tail's shadow better than tail.
His eyes, still blue, were dim come dark.

And bear with Julian who, blue-eyed in his third year,
launched a kitten against the kitchen wall.
He saw nothing far of the consequences,
no more than our extravagantly lethal youth
unleashed abroad with bomb, napalm and naked blade.
Nor I know mine.
And yet I act.
I journey, beget, I chide the child, compose this verse
in my grave Ausonian summer,
in the death-rip of an empire
countervail an act of sound against the sufficient void.

Out of but so little Julian acts:
taking a first step, who might not crush an ant,
while second steps could crack the world's back.
Except for that page in Barnabe Barnes I skipped,
except for the truck I missed

139

out of the Brazilian backlands,
except for the touched petal-flare of cyclamen
and other axiological modalities,
would I commit this venture against the dark?

The kitten, along with his sister, survived
long enough to acquire an extravagant name;
but shortly after both died of creeping ringworm
that flourished largely due to our neglect.

BATTLEGROUND

I found an appeasable place
to plant my immortelles,
by moon's composing light
according to spells.

Men came at dawn with wheat
and made it their domain.
Remembering naked bread,
I couldn't complain.

Processional at sunset
came the hunger-bred
to trample down the grain
and bury their dead.

Now that weather's wintry
there's somewhere we should go,
but we still wait for flowers,
for song from the crow.

HOW THEY HUNT THE QUICK RED FOX

Always the fox gets caught, yet not by skill
so much as through the beast's acute disdain
for huntsmen who retard the chase until
the quarry, suffering freedom on the brain,
stops to survey them lagging up some hill.

Yoiks! they halloo, but hint at paradox,
for though they share one ritual, they loot
each one a various hunt, a different fox,
not the slaying but for aye pursuit,
their hour for what it moves and not for clocks.

Nor do they cherish the hound with reddest chin,
packrat fondled and as straight despised,
that would not straggle but in venal din
plunders the desire that most they prized
and in the rucksack substitutes chagrin.

MAY MORNING ADMONITION

This morning tigress Snookums creeps on the porch
eyeing a bird on a magnolia branch,
Snookums born in the market of Veracruz,
a stranger to Louisiana, swishes
her tail in time to heartbeats. Then the bird,
gauging, enjoying distance every inch,
meows with magnificent one-upmanship,
startling our monster almost out of her skin.
O mockingbird, you shouldn't ought to do it.
Ripeness is all: birds and blossoms in God's time
fall, whether He be blossom, bird, or cat.

THE ERRANT MOLE AND THE LOVELIEST OF HAWKS

for Bud Olderman

Sparrow-spry, the orgiastic barnyard
rejoices in its zion gone to seed.
Was it such brutal stamping on dirt packed hard
brought the mole up to blunder against weed,
or self-collisions felt round each blunt corner
where storms of clods discharged a dense pressure?

Well, whatever, the hills are stubble-brown,
troughs are green, and the mole in open air,
like country cousin erupted on the town,
is caught up in a fluent everywhere,
while sassafras, whose single root he knew,
displays in leaf three shapes and contacts now.

I somehow apprehend his heliotrope
is porcelain, his trumpet-flower-red
is thorny, and fragrance is a seismoscope
attesting his old home redistributed.
Soon he conceives of the hawk, a Cimmerian
borne from the hills on wings that chill the sun,

god's messenger if not the god full-fledged.
Since contact is his only armament,
he antics on a heap with no bets hedged,
conspicuously prey, and confident
that it will be the loveliest of hawks,
he be forgiven the apostolic hoax.

Later, after I had watched my fill
of terror and possession under the claw,
taxing me beyond my mortal skill
to keep down vision, given what I saw,
I found it warped me out of mind to crawl
into that hide no bigger than my soul.

GREAT HIGH FEASTS ON THE BIRTHDAYS
OF LITTLE MEN

No poet should admit to limitation:
       every prior is a pope;
between may lie illimitable relation,
       yet there precisely lives our hope.

Side issues coining merit, we go for broke;
       example: our antithetical
contracts with society provoke
       daemonic aplomb to shock and brawl.

Vocation's not weighed-in by quantity
       nor is it hungering relative.
Never do vocation and faculty
       cannibalize each other to live.

FAREWELL TO BAEDEKER

La Antigua, Veracruz

Totonac and Colonial
and near the rank plaza a tree:
so ruins have their say to me,
for I am falling in their fall.

The village, no trophy of the age
nor quite a hostage to the map
(albeit an "archeological site"),
will never make a ruin, will blow
off in oblivion's eye, its church
dust, not relic, with cobbled streets
wide as houses tall, with grackles
posing in the mango trees
instead of fruit, walls opalescent
with damp, landscape, inscape, lostscape,
dust all, no token returned, for even
the words on their irretrievable way
to silence will be lost.
      Totonac
blood demanded pyramid
and sacrificial altar; blood
flashes from bush to bush, and my hand
with having brushed this death is ice
on posterity; and yet my skin
does not prickle, for even the gods
have now abandoned these monuments.

Does ruin, unlike flower and tree,
change when flags are changed?

                                   Antique
baronial violence has fetched
nothing here to unhinge my knee,
since by the gods abandoned. The whole
of a wordless yore, repeated in me,
is execration deformed by calm
where sandstone echoes crumble in wind,
an antiquary's cackle.

                                  The tree,
felled by who cares what cataclysm,
since lightning, earthquake, hurricane
concerted to deracinate
this ruinous deity, now lies
flat, and wider than houses tall,
an ancient sight. I pay no peso
to feel the high-borne leaf (laid low
yet ready centuries to hand)
unhand me, terrifyingly green.

ANTAEUS

The giant fall of a jungle ceiba,
half-rotten deacon of silences
held close by lliana and a wrestling
fig, such hungry witnesses,

becomes a purgatorial moment
lengthened out by noon. At first,
hear hushing after the trunk's cracking,
or vacuum brimming with all worst,

a wuthering rush, the rising storm
and swell of a multitudinous scurry,
of monkey chatter and jay screech,
emergent civilization and hurry

before the crash, then reel with earth's
staggering under what thunder brings.
Where the ceiba stood tall the sky
hovers, one only parrot for wings.

WORDS WITH NORMAN ROSTEN

We fling our being, Norman, hurl our full flesh
smack against the blank wall of our mysteries
as though to burst through and to burst through,
as though to leave as signature a hole
and leave our shattered selves on the far side,
never the near side, not so near the start.
Our sign's a bloodied brow.
For a time we feel we're passing through,
are on neither side, and that the darkness
is the substance of being immured in stone;
yet know no wall can be this thick. We're still
hurling ourselves, but are a little inured
to impact, now.

ACADEMY OF SINCERITY

Fat robin redbreast getting fatter,
pecking choke-cherries off a tree,
encores till heart or belly bursts,
yet that's not sincerity.

There's our amorist a-mooning;
his heart, unzipped for all to see,
slides on the steel of his guitar,
yet that's not sincerity.

Here's an artist who imagines
chaos into something free
and formed, fervent with various thought,
yet that's not sincerity.

Inside's a ferment whose defenses
privily claim, "This *this* is me"
yet knows that this is insincere,
and there's frank-pledged sincerity.

LULLABY FOR NOW

Now fear, the engine of all turnaround,
no longer need defend you on your way:
sleep loose who through the livelong-leery day
tightened at every unaccustomed sound.
Now, my good assassin, cover your crime
with commemorative ivy, so death-begone
in the primal pause of fear, so put upon
last year, the Year of the Caesars, the sleep in slime.
Now sleep, and dream how in this lullaby
you last an instant of what fills a life
in city, building, rubble, speck in eye,
and how your monstrous powers can obtain
poems and light from fear and rest from strife
in body, rot, liquescence, cloud, clean rain.

THE POET'S PRESCRIPTION OF SHAMELESSNESS

Tell me, my dear, what wasteful sense
would make you marshal self's defense
      behind a cough
and cause me to study reticence
or print instead of sacraments
      when clothes are off?

Let's find the means to humble shame,
or, giving the devil his modern name,
      inhibitions;
let's wince from nothing save to blame
fears and throes that threaten fame
      with admonitions.

As intimate we two must get
as any man and woman yet
      if I'm to know you.
Indulge the freaks my notions whet
while I your fantasies abet.
      Come, I'll show you.

And then there's rest. Then recognize
this face buried between your thighs
      without a trap.
Our bodies' wisdoms thus advise
that, naked, we give a naked guise
      congenerous sap.

HAIKU

You are the bright bird
burning on the golden bough
of my erection.

&

The perfect balance
between your right and left breasts
is my vertigo;

the fine imbalance
between your right and left thighs
shoots my vision home.

THE CAMELLIA

By the bushful I have known camellias,
on the rose of all winds blown, abandoned, possessed,
by blue light, red light, yellow, slate and starlight,
in gardens, poems, amongst luxuriant breasts.

In Ipanema, in a garden, once,
a bilocation (brought to touch and sight
when a fern's probe of brewing space was denied
by pine needles) was bathed in camellias' light.

But one camellia, clearest by desert light,
dark leaves protesting against Natal's noon glare,
by holding a nipply brown stain to its lip
locks me in hard responsive flint. I dare

the beginning of rot, perhaps, tacit the bane,
and I, a prodigal son, will never forget
how sundown, riding on the rim of heat,
browned that venereal blemish deeper yet.

I sifted clouds for a fatted calf; the sun
dropped its barred wheel through the unlocked gate
of sand, of bush. And still the white flesh glowed.
The stain, distinct from night, accumulates.

THE SMALL RAIN

Shyly it sprinkles, every drop a girl,
    a pattering to panes; four times
    it stops, starts, stops, then spatters a swirl
of indecisive and diffident paradigms.

But when the pane becomes one driving sheet
    of wild waters in the gusts
    that lash them, who am I to meet
her thrusting swollen to avail my thrusts?

COSTA RICAN PASTORAL

Rain squalls on afternoon's tin roof,
crabgrass globed, poinsettia heavy
along a fence's broken slats,
tatters of banana leaves
shredding the sky, beneath them red-ripe
coffee berries, river heaving
toward fruit: a young girl, halving the road
at a wide angle, struts, as dark
as brewed coffee, on her pert head
the basket of teats she calls papayas,
under her skin the blood flared up.
Does the writing of words suffice
against the heat, against the chill
when teeth and hair are leaching away?
A goat sheltered by a stilt-root,
rubbing his itch on curls of whitewash,
under him, cluckingly dry, a hen.
I fling an emptied shell at the girl
against the chill, against the heat.
She came to my door, in out of the rain.
My mind again tumescent with words.

PATIO

A swallow, noiseless as a shadow,
darts about her half a saucer
of crumbling clay and bamboo slivers.
Jasmine fragrances and flicker
of poinciana intertwine
with custard apples bursting rinds
on my spinal trellis. From the *calle*
tequila curses and poverty swings
a murderous machete. I try
rendering a chorale, a round,
enticing the swallow in the dusk,
but am surprised there by my son
who questions why I sing alone.

STAR-APPLE

I cut it in two and give the child,
staring, famished, the larger piece.
She eats in great gulps, making up,
glorying in its stickiness.
For half an hour I contemplate
the pattern of mine, the tracery
of dark on lighter grey, surrounded
by purple to shame an emperor.
But in the end I eat it, too,
glorying in its stickiness.

LIFELINE TRAIN TO PUERTO LIMÓN

Rumble-rattle, rumble-rattle,
steel and cattle, numb with battle,
crumb and water, want and chattel,
rumble-rattle, rumble-rattle.

Shrunken a woman grey to her shawl
shares with me the rush and haul
jungle flashes outside by
flower and fruit bewilder the eye.

Wheels constricting starving lives
pass cacao in sumptuous hives
pass bananas pass the trees
that pass through sawmills pass police,

the whistle whoos, the wheels click-click
calling the pinched, the grim, the sick
to lift its loads, to cringe and borrow,
leaving to din again tomorrow.

Rumble-rattle, rumble-rattle,
numb as cattle, sick of battle,
rumble-rattle, want and chattel,
sick so sick so sick so sick . . .

CALENTURES

Out picking cowslips on the meadows of the sea,
    down gradual billows grassy as my youth,
        I do not feel the tow turn mean,
            the fever in my bones.

Horizon-bound, a ship's hull rots in its own lea.
    St. Elmo scarifies old Jonah's youth.
        Ragged sails glare and lean.
          Oysterous ocean groans.

How alarming, these cowslips, in their fragility,
    how heavy, heavy my hand yellowed with youth!
        Only the whale's belly comes between
          my fever and my bones.

NOW ARE WE REMEMBERED

She spoke, dwelling upon me from restraint:

"I, parch-bearer in the transient, have you at last.
Ragged my eyes were raised to the stinging year,
wasp-year hiving not even hearsay of you; but at last
I've my near voice of you: your hair, your mouth.
Overlaying the land, I was dust, and brooded
through disparaged rain for your sake, protested
jays to define nothing-to-echo ceilings.
Came the multitudes, saluting me with seed
which in my womb mildewed, blight-begetting,
lacking you. And I have fathomed how flanks,
presumptive of arid homage, shrivel up, turn blue.
Only, I could not die, could precinct my cloak
but tighter about me. Lying so, I dreamt
you almsgave love's blade, I embraced a rime
keen enough to shred the air. It shuddered
at my loins, oh wintry up to the clinging hilt,
but your hand that could cede it warmth prescinded
—how many drouths ago? And when I rose to my feet,
what, who dispersed me, flakes from a blistered sky.
Now I, who could not brook to be your echo,
neither sunlight paling out your shadow,
now am I remembered to your sorrow."

Beloved, I cried, beloved, all through your storming
I was its center bled to a waging peace;
beloved, I cried, beloved, I served the main-chance,
vigilant from what time violets (who were nuns
in leaf-wet keeps) learned to interpret light askance
until the aster's under-a-toadstool spell of stiff scurvy,
I was a sandgrain immensely lost in you,
preserving one small seed to give you back
if you would only speak, if you would only speak.

SHARING IT WITH ANGELS

Half-light, appalled, blinked when I said,
"I have my share of love and of more than love",
    implying: What are you thinking of
to dare the beckonings of a word as dead
    as chivalry? It's in my head
to modify the muddle to *more than share;*
    but, bluntly, isn't the error in *more,*
as though both loving and sharing were some lore
    that overwrites our simple care?

Blink away, half-glimmer gone mad
    with darkness. Angels batter my gate.
More than your most, they know what love's about.
    They know because they never doubt
    my earnest lights. Oh, love's a sad
devil when it sets its lamps on fate
        and cries, "Out! Out!"

165

RACHEL AND LEAH

"One shape of many names"
— Shelley

Jacob, double-tongued with Rachel and farmy Leah,
    wrestled less in his thigh's hour woman
        than wings in a night
          of flight:
        wind-chilled through an idea
    in which the knotty roots of seven human
years lie shriveled, no feast for uxorious appetite.

Outcropping gestures pile a level countryside
    thought-high, buckling escarpments meant
        to cripple the third
          sought word,
        a climbing word whose bride
    is granite. So our sons must travel bent
double, forking what dream in Rachel's womb is stirred.

But travel where? A Chinese sage, his centuries
    ago, lay dreaming butterflies
        his panacea.
          Was he a
        bridler of the breeze
    or at its mercy till he wakes and dies?
Did Jacob dream that Leah was Rachel and Rachel Leah?

He finds a jot of each in every day's surprise
    and loses some in every throng;
        but she who became
          the tame
        slack shanks and worried eyes
    of Leah, the bride intended all along,
is who, invoked as Rachel, eagers to that name.

THE SEASONS IN A LANDSCAPE OF WOMAN

Blue under sky and green under trees —
I wonder what my lovely sees.

I saw a film of colors take
to bone and crystal for her sake.

Cocked to the muffled clashing of spears —
I wonder what my darling hears.

I heard a stunned remembrance roar,
the solace of one, one hour more.

In her stiff hair she crushes a rose —
I wonder what my darling knows.

I know an hour that turns to two,
I tend the fire but slip on dew.

White under trees, black under ground —
I wonder what my lovely found.

LINES TO A WHITE PERSIAN SLEEPING

White pool, draining out beneath a star-apple,
I, who skin my own teeth puzzling over the stakes
driven through sleep's buried heart, discern a fealty
in lightless lightning starting at your rear right paw
(opening on its stalk like some carnivorous flower)
and reaving the sinews of your shoulder's arch of triumph
to halt propitiated, low, near where your vigil's lit.
White pool, I shore it all now, share it watching
earth soak you up under the fountaining star-apple.

ENIGMA OF A FINAL SCENE

Across his eyes the mourners lay
a woman's well-worn pelvic bone,
yet Don Juan cannot rightly say,
floating on down, if he has known
the wench or not: under a sark
it's all the same dead-heat in the dark.

Thus adust to Hades. Gluttony
and squalor uphold those glittery halls,
a grand hotel's cheap luxury
whereof his senses are the walls
synoptic to groans from serried beds
and gnashing dust in chattering heads.

There a woman, hectic, bleak,
is given him that she may blow
his embers till he lies so weak
he'd perish in his ashes, no
fulfillment in her Juan-shaped eyes
albeit his hell's her paradise.

GOING TOO FAR

Discover it not so easy (oh, I do!
I do!) to come upon your loves so soon
unloving, loving easeful grope and rue,
loving desert, deserting wind and dune.

Alone they came; they fling away in throngs;
they rupture, like amoeba, staying all;
yet all's too little, yr weals, yr wails, yr wrongs,
their doom and drama rictused on a fall.

All is sooner lost than most renewed.
Do you take these partly whole, this who?
And answer, speaking as many having pursued
disparagement to hell, I do! I do!

THE DOCTOR WILL BE BACK TOO LATE

Because I was hungrier than sleepy,
she hooked me into conjugating again,
the third time. Then it was light,
the window turning blue. I thought
she glowed in the dark:
I might have lit a Pall Mall at her nipple.

When the chancy bones have slipped
undulating Venus her due,
contingent snares are suddenly tripped
and head over heals the thrust is new.

I bit into an apple so firm
it crunched back at me its red and white
defiance. The light is dirty,
gritty. When Ovid is God's mouthpiece
the hours get longer
all the year long, and the bones melt apace.

My mouth tastes like a buzzard's nest.
The Great Ginsboyg and even moreso Corso
come to me in *The Times*
to rile with old puerilities.
As one poet
put it, "The cast of characters never changes."

Behind her kiss I feel a face
shattered by bombs across the seas
cradles rock a violent race;
I can't believe her expertise.

Like money, sperm's a detriment
unless you spend it. Recalling bright orange
monkey-flow'rs, I think:
oh, orange is a screaming woman!
"What a grey day,"
she says. "We might as well go back to sleep."

YOUNG GRIMSHAW

Rook Grimshaw posed the problem neat:
"When losses tot by tot return
are they restored as loss or gain?"
He spoke of his wife, a liar and cheat.

His rival: "When the gambler's bread
floats home, though legal tender be other,
what does the treasury care? Why bother
with value if you're not in the red?"

"They say returns restore tenfold.
Surely that's a replete sum of naught
to entertain in a house still fraught
concretely—double-dyed fool's gold."

Axman proposed a telic worth:
"With resignation's stomach, learn
to swallow what can let you turn
gall and chagrin to honey and mirth."

"But resignation's vacant, too,"
Grimshaw grinned at the trees, "a value
solemnly zeroed in on zero.
And yet, — what else can prodigal do?"

"Try soothsay with the fatted calf.
Its entrails, webbed across your mind,
will comfort, yearning, its own kind,
while at your hub you bloat and laugh."

Grimshaw, dodging Axman, gripped
his mind until his heart bled white:
"Even Gyges lacked your wit;
but I'm afraid its ring is clipped."

When Grimshaw disappeared, the note
impersonated a suicide.
Why didn't Axman think so? "Pride
had nothing there to grip by the throat."

MILLAIS LOQUACIOUS

The one book able to give me stable advice
on how to conduct this crisis in my life,
Montaigne, I think, or some such incontestable voice,
    I'd hidden on my dustiest shelf,
unthinkingly on purpose, without impulse or fuss,
    then grumbled whenever I came across it.
    I'd turned my mind off like a faucet.

Unthinkingly I flushed out John, I think,
who shrewdly indicated old Montaigne.
It struck me at once, with a faint, a self-absorbing thunk,
    John was needed to ascertain
what well I knew; but he'd have me, his friend, to thank.
    In fact, I couldn't abide the book.
    John is the man whose wife I took.

TO THE DISCREET READER: AN INDUCTION
TO INDISCRETIONS

We must at times acknowledge on the balance sheet:
    the winning part of wisdom's indiscreet.
The man who, serving his neighbor's wife, spreads the report,
    will serve the neighborhood in matching sort.
Such indiscretions as the instance here betrayed
    are testimonials of a renegade
less to his loves than to a cold, forbidding art
    that disavows the bard who serves his heart.
Such hearts revenge themselves, begetting on a crone,
    while wives will swear they rumpled the bed alone.

LINES UPON DELIA AND TO THE CHEVALIERS
OF THE CORDON BLEU

When Delia fair defleas her bitch
or rids poor puss of scabs and scales,
or digs her crotch to soothe an itch,
where does it go but under the nails?

Nothing's to gain inventing excuses!
Celestial airs will turn full gales
to blab out what the actual news is.
Where can it go but under the nails?

Fantastic how she swipes at her crupper
and misses betimes! It seldom fails
some ends in breakfast, some in supper
For where did it go but under the nails?

She gnaws her nails, and it is this
that Strephon savors in their kiss.

RECONSTRUCTION

Red lips, green eyes, black hair.
Were Proteus to praise
illapsable constancy,
fate by strictly opposing would share,
not be conditioning, yesterdays.
Proteus, though, is prophecy.
I saw the same red, green and black elsewhere
before your birth: your mother's photo decays,
yours thrives; and yet, you are the same as she.
Where does the daughter trip that the mother does not fare?
Or what belongings claim the one the other can't declare?
Tree, mould, coal, diamond, my love — nothing stays,
my dear. A nereid's eyes, while you and I are kissing, glaze
and smooth the bearded salt. Were your virginity
what you suppose, intact, where did you steal your pedigree?

TO PEG

Give me some luck, sweet Peg,
rub against me, your leg
trembling under my hand.
So bodies will understand
the long and the short of it
and spirit will learn to love it.
O Peg, it's far from luck!
It's will: my mind got struck
in virtue, beauty, a bed
where the better is bred,
where St. Augustine shows
how weeds become a rose,
the scale of our perfection
taking a true direction.

INQUEST

Tiresias, having squinted into your ingle,
I know the sordid bungle: how the snake,
enraged when you dispatched his blissom tangle,
changed you spindlewise, and lent you your knack
for harlotry; and how deep Athena's torn
Erichthonius off her shield to foil
your foe; and laps your hearing so you'll learn
the vulgate of fate's prophetic dark fowl.
I've spilled my libations to Persephone.
So now there's lamb's blood in the trench to float
argosies, all because you're reputed wise.
But damn it! when you advise me I must let
the sun-cattle of Hyperion be!
What? Even when they stray into her eyes?

THE LAYING-OUT OF LAZARUS

Gently the women have spread me naked on linen.
Martha and Mary are unabashed, but the servants
goggle when my wife turns her back. Soft-handed,
slicked with olibanum and camphor, they knead me,
fingers slipping in and out of my oxters,
suppling the horny, stroking the furfur lustrous.
As I grow colder and imminently formless,
they knead me warm.

She who never in traffics and ages of marriage
groped for my rod, oh neither with love nor with malice,
lingers now a moment there; yet my body,
unctuous in its afterwit, grows colder,
analgesic to perfervid tokens,
rich because for self it wishes nothing.
Were I brought back, I, God-helped Eleazar,
God! I'd scream!

CIRCE

Though I prefer to charm my solitude with animals,
        wet monkey fur, goat smells,
    do men adore me less, or at my cup their flesh
        less submit to its backlash?
For they have found not to unmake me but accept from my hand,
        to follow my heels behind
    or rumple against my flanks when I descend to greet
        salvage the tides have brought.
They come dumped from pig-snouted prows, a bestial, murderous load.
        We gad a green glade,
    clamp jaws on meat; but what attends me in their eyes
        no fondling will appraise,
they being glazed eyes, grunting, rutted and trampled down in mire
        and they will die no more
    because the metamorphosis against my lean
        heart fails, and I am alone.

A DOUBLE BALLADE OF NEWFANGLED LADIES

for La Martinelli

Where is that Helen, who could occupy
Egypt and Troy at once, and yet succumb
to the inchmeal time memorials certify?
Or Cleopatra's honied, silken thumb
that burnt the topless towers at Actium
and left a print for time to venerate?
Show me Helena, Simon Magus' mate,
who claims in Helen's person to inhere,
then I'll show that which time must propagate.
Last winter's snows will snow again this year.

Where are the basilisks that edify
unless they kill, that in opprobrium
and aureate bestiality deny
for all time; Pasiphaë who through her dumb
encounter lashed Athenian valor numb?
Semiramis who bore a stallion's weight?
Messalina? Theodora? Great,
perfidious, apostate Guinevere
who snowed her king's court under its ghostly fate?
Last winter's snows will snow again this year.

Does Lesbia, her womb all Rome's ripe sty,
hop after her sparrow still, feasting on love's crumb
down that long yew-shaded road, or vie
with Cynthia to farrow delirium?
Where's Baudelaire's black-haunted vacuum?
Or Beatrice, through whom we consecrate

the light which Laura's loins will not abate?
Or she whose ruthless broom sings mighty and clear,
Blake's household Muse, I mean his dearest Kate?
Last winter's snows will snow again this year.

Was Daphne cut, is Arethusa dry,
Syrinx turned to coal? Has Christendom
hounded bright Callisto from the sky?
What barrens bloom, beholding Hagar come?
Where's Tamar? And Dido, toppler of Carthage? From
whose tomb does amazed Lucretia supplicate?
Where does Inés de Castro dissipate
the sovereignty and occult hemisphere
of Death, presiding from her equal state?
Last winter's snows will snow again this year.

And Ruth? And Rachel? Death, did Rachel die?
And tell me, what of Antigone, the sum
of credible virtues, where do her relics lie?
And sublime Zenobia, rare as radium?
And was Vittoria Colonna's viaticum
a final grace? Yet, who should dedicate
Rahab's thighs to ruin's precipitate,
or Phryne's nards and rouge, and be severe
because Ninon at ninety was not sedate?
Last winter's snows will snow again this year.

Where does raving Cassandra bewilder her cry,
to Troy and to her darkness burdensome,
where is her spirit nerved to prophesy
her city's death? Where now does Judith plumb
one wound as coldly-terrored as Ilium
with all its thousands, whose beauty opened the gate

184

drowning the locusts of Assur in its spate?
Oh, where's Saint Joan, who rose with chanticleer
because an angel's fury must not wait?
Last winter's snows will snow again this year.

L'Envoi

Villon, from between my lines disintricate
those women form could not incorporate.
Seas, rivers, lakes and puddles persevere
alive with them: ask little; but look straight.
Last winter's snows will snow again this year.

PIETÀ

Two women folding a double mystery
—for how could one sustain it?—bend as one.

Two women weeping: once for the agony
just ended; once for the load of woe begun
just now, which He submits to silently
until the glad Descent is reified
at the bitter heel of temporal history.

Which oracle's the most momentous bride?
One woman is the mother of God in man,
the other lover of man in God. The first,
because she's plighted to the child she nursed;
the second, since she was a harlot, can
contain the grievous man's ubiquity.

Their faces, glimmering toward me in the name
of God and daily darkness, are the same.

ALL I WANTED TO SAY

I love you. That is all I wanted to say.
But somewhere in the telling failure betrays
the saying, so I remark on foul weather
and how the mare and stallion snapped their tethers

during the night. Beneath your blouse your nipples
harden and glow as the tongue of fable prods
you down an empty aisle. That minute's god
has laughed a year or more to maim a cripple.

A simple declaration's dialectics
crosshatch and boobytrap our minds with hectic
words returning to their source alone.
Every day more people blab to stones.

From

SOME SIGNS VISIBLE BEFORE BEFORE

JUDGMENT

(1980)

THIS BOOK IS FOR HARRIETTE

Forgive me if, forgetful now and again
in what church I've had leave to pray
or which bell summons to creation's praise,
forgive me, love, that sometimes I have made
of your sage flesh a pulpit to show forth
some signs visible before judgment.
Remit the wine, condone the shattered cup:
one day they will hark back to you, all things
of the immanent many-mansioned love
forward into the past for you,
O broken vessel's pattern known
not least amid that broken company
of generous witnesses (for though we slept
on the wing's hunger, within me ever I felt
you brushing either side), not less than Laura
nor any remembered auspice under the coiled sun
and oh! lips will be lips and no less the swallow return!

WALKING WITH ANGELS

for Everette & Franz

Whoever you may be, however endowed,
you know the dangling strain that youth may bear
if you have walked with angels unaware,
what though they stepped out roundly, self-avowed,
and one has brought you safely through the crowd
(that makes a shambles of the thoroughfare)
into your solitude, a silence where
your awe can grip the leap from groin to cloud.
His healing stroke is at the desert well
most faithfully shown, for there you're given time
to feature yourself, then drop a stone below;
thus, out of discomposure, rounds propel
your face against the crumbling walls of lime,
and, when you're most alone, he lets you go.

INVERSION FACTOR

Standing on his hands, he takes no walk.
There is nowhere else to go but here
isolated between heaven and earth,
strict between not-any-more and not-yet
that handicap his now, his flight, dream-flight
as work of waking, waiting for that birth.

There had been, lately, crisis in our times.
Unprofitable war — the nation's, his own —
petitioned then exacted sacrifice
to reverse established versions: bullet or stone
into ideal thought, self-discipline
into compliance, virtue consulting vice.

Although he keeps his fingers crossed, his blood
spills through an hourglass waist into his head,
while feet in concentrated headwork wave
like the antennas of the fly on his nose
until a twitching makes him recognize
that Virtue had been better off a Knave.

Legs, in such dislocation, cannot frame
the topsy-turvy view which queerly corrects
a queerer correction native to his head,
so branches are roots arrested in the sky,
hills drift down from clouds, and steadily
landscape is suffused with whoozy red.

Such metamorphoses of martyrdom
into the evermore of ecstasy
are titans bound and into chaos hurled.
And though his palms go sinking down through dirt,
and there's a vulture auguring on his gut,
in his illusion he supports the world.

THE FIRST ROW

Not to encroach on Abel's herds
was surely least of Cain's restraints.
But gusto for blood, offense of blood
in crisp air needled by tamarisks,
got him sick once, so it occurs
disgust invents the plow. He hymns:
O heart, my body's winepress, work
in me no awe to stay my hand,
but let me start this row. For man,
hunter born, his arms the crowd
and solitude his prey, restricts
his shadow to its palisades
but not his thumbs from offending earth.
His plow is heavy, his balance poor
though wealthy in possibilities;
his plow is clumsy, would tip him off
and tickle him down the unfended field.
Are there ways out, and would those ways
be his own way? Or would they appear
thrust of another's abandonment?
He hesitates on an edge, his body
(seeded with mocking bones) no answer.
Already the spear of the first horseman
topping the rise suggests to him
he must defend his plumes of grain.
His torso, merely to do, trips
forward, overbalanced perhaps,
out of sheer impetus plows on
in and out of the wilderness.

TRANSLATED FROM SILENCE

He spreads pale lids to make the mirror jump,
yet since his gaze abhors from quitting his eyes
he does not see the usual room, his wife
so still in the cyclone of her chair, the lamb
laughing in the hearth that ruddies the glass.

He treads, between the forest and the field,
a vast periphery in vaster snow,
a silence centuries in the drifting down.
Echo's asleep in the circle of somber larch trees
whose tips seem furze about to disappear.

Ages gone his belling hounds sank down.
The hunter strides on, aimed and cocked in purpose,
with boots, the shoulders of his black and red
plaid jacket, crusted, epauletted with snow.
He steps and stoops and stops his zodiac.

The stag, in noble antlers renewed, is not
ignoble just because he can't be seen
devoting swiftness to the rims of vision.
Neither is there a crow. There's nothing as dark
as the black hearts of snow-devils beating.

He steps and stoops and deepens, the hunter. Tracks
close in a stopped circumference at whose
hub his cabin hunches, huddles. There
cold clinkers outstare ashes, there his wife's
a skeleton in her unmoving chair.

Neither on the horizon nor at the zenith
(where footstep leaves no track) appears the stag,
for this is motion for its own sake's doom.
Flakes rise fumbling for the hunter's mouth.
They do not fill it, though they are endless, endless.

AGAIN I'M TORCHED AND WONDER
WHAT WE'VE WROUGHT

Self

Again I'm torched in one of those grandiose
suttees of our soul in search of her body,
lighting up with her death an object-life
that otherwise could hold no dialogue.
The sacrifice of this demanding wife,
as always, leaves our intellect agog.

Soul

I am the circle squared in that I test
nonbeing in the being of nonbeing.
My quest is fire and so no sacrifice
except on evidence; my words engrave
our body's skin with grooves of risky advice.
You are presumptuous if we think I save.

Body

My record plays the song that angels hear,
but in a scratchy version. Head to toes
my skin's tattooed. The circus gels are bright
on battlefields of hearts & flowers in choir
where all my characteristics reunite.
And then one noon the big top catches fire.

Intellect

The strain of bringing all together cracks
my self-sufficiency at primal times
of immolation. Still, I abide my laws;
I query faithfully till circle-come,

striving to comprehend the siren's cause
and set her full return *ad libitum*.

Self

We burn together; I'm engraved, amazed,
and think I strain it all together. The thought
is not my own — yet so it seems. Unrazed,
I speak for each, and wonder what we've wrought.

THE PROPHETS

Neither sinners nor saints, their visions maintain
the balance we would otherwise so lack,
since weights nonplus, awhirl like a weathervane,
and prickle like a stare behind your back.

Whether in Jonah, the classical comical Jew,
or fury's Jeremiah, in mystical
Ezekiel, or any poet who
but dare, the gift is antediluvial,

a manner of telling cradles from the sudd:
I, too, with boozy Noah in his ark
sailed the insulting Asiatic flood
and nine months boiled in a maiden's spastic dark

with nowhere in this sweat of a world to go
except where I was rapt by words. Their source
is their fulfilledness compelled to sow
stubborn tundras with prophetic force,

their flayed-skin dispensation stripped from time
that's less the future's vapor than the past's
surplus of detritus, a skein of slime
on harborage and roadstead, keel to masts.

Though seers may be unlike in how they burn,
at sea and in womb their will's anonymous,
contracting to the prick of all return
by rendering history superfluous.

Such foolish beards, hilarious jokes on time,
jutting out at eternal sunsets, taint
bread they break, accuse them of the crime
of non-complicity: no sinner, no saint.

Now I am ready. Awesome I advance
to where the tyrant drains glass after glass.
I thunder, prophetic lightning in my glance,
and face them under the table, eating grass.

WRESTLING WITH ANGELS

for Robert Jurgrau

What an amazing thing to watch a man
   of property, a patriarch
   admired for early making his mark,
wrestle all night like any barbarian,

but with no visible antagonist;
   with tangibles as of temperature;
   with thrust a pressure, as it were,
of wonderment bearing down on his wrist!

To see him see himself in the adversary's
   eyes: the wrestler in plain sight grows
   younger, softer, as one who knows
not youth again but how a mirror tarries.

A dense black light of touch illuminates
   unalterable blessings renewed;
   from now on he is iron-thewed,
his wound and victory integral traits.

Shouts and groans perhaps for a later day,
   a later destruction with trumpet roar
   and crashing walls, are held in store:
now, hear a locust scores of miles away.

Your shuttered magics will record no more
   when in reversals of your loss
   at last it comes your turn to cross
that space between the river and the shore.

ONE OF THE OLD ONES

for Simon Perchik

Man's full console of cries, his howls and whines,
his yelps, grunts, groans, and arias of a life
that compounds love but lets the interest go,
his noisy objections, rank rejections, call
each to an order he can never know.
A central noise, note well, his central silence,
is plain in Thoreau's "quiet desperation,"
a bottommost roaring sun.
                        The scene: a tower,
a figure watching, strident at the top.
A tank of water breathes pelagic hush.
Silence, really, is both scene and act.
The water subsides, rises, laps your eyes
as though a tear must answer to the sea
and the high inpour magnetized mere tanks.
Then, ghostly, portending from the limpid depths,
a thunderhead of unknowing reifies
against the glass. This is no time for tears,
screeches, squalls, brawls, brays, hisses, whimpers, shrieks.
Observe, painstakingly, elusive eyes
in the lateral lobed expansions of the head,
called hammerhead; acknowledge the protoplasmic
coloration, perhaps a dream gone sick,
and the fin slicing through awakening.
In short, see if you can learn to know it
from outside in — sustain the silence of it
once inside — or through its interfusion
with water, through water, desperate for the sea.
While quiet edges fray to hubbub, note
the hammerhead, it smashes your skull, and mark
how partially it partakes of reality
till it blunts its snout against your thought of yourself.

THE SWIFT COMPLETION OF THEIR
APPOINTED ROUNDS

"The horror! The horror!"
       – Heart of Darkness

I sit secreted in the dark
security of a cupboard crack.
Only hunger cautions me apart
      from what I lack,

hunger and that biting light.
Fragility of existence, offset
by patience and tenacity, imply
      some lurking debt,

although to whom I can't conceive.
Begat on the crumb on which I thrive,
I do not scruple devouring my progeny
      to stay alive:

whatever fattens will return —
wallpaper paste, garbage, grain.
We are as old as anything on earth.
      I will remain.

I'll feast on my totalities.
Or should I scurry from this place,
trusting implications not to reveal
      my carapace?

No, I burn in a darkened fire.
A morsel of offal for a lever.
I move the ages to suit me: I'll survive
      replete forever.

II

ROCOCO BIRDBATH WITH FIGURINE OF
DAPHNE AS WARNING TO VIRGINS

No nightingale: water, dense, still;
wind, drugged in festooned moonlight,
slumbers in water up to his hilt.

Here a chase, in play begun
by light delinquent in a grove,
is lapsing in a semblance of

Daphne, half in leafage, half
in that nearer change, that nubile grace
that now will never come to pass.

With eyes of inconclusive clout,
liquid with love, kindled with scorn,
and lips between a laugh and frown,

she twists towards whom the basin reflects:
exhaustion stiffens through the bronze
as laurel, clasping a cold flank, says . . .

MAN-GIRAFFE

My rival, obscurely effeminate,
not like a girl, more like a giraffe,
at home in James or Proust, yet half
lost in mimosas, delicate

on hinges that waltz him among the trees,
is awkwardness with grace combined.
Giraffe in him engrossing my mind,
I quite neglect my woman's ease.

His figure in the carpet is grass;
he, chary as he prints his feet,
recoils from spirits and from meat,
yet nibbles and accepts a glass.

When fangs of orchids force his hide
or breezes disconcert his trek,
murder's implied in the sway of his neck
so gently it seems a suicide;

and horizon in his gaze invokes
savannas where the grass springs rife,
while mountain roots of valley life
infer him one of the gracious jokes

whose loping ripples along a course
would shatter teacups if he veered.
Yet, when far off they disappeared,
my woman rode him like a horse.

THE MAN WHO WAS PREGNANT WITH ENVY

You centered in on one you could not stand,
a trans-idea, meta-sentiment
who dressed his figure and a side of beef
with equal pomp. But being no malcontent,
how could you tell when envy preempted grief?
There's but so much one man can understand.

That you were getting big with child was clear.
And clearly to be pregnant's to be so
with other, though the speckling of that thing
may be such stuff as thinking cannot know.
Amniotic cloudburst-heads, that cling
to you like milkweed, make all else unclear.

You keep an ear cocked at the thing's closed door.
Hardly could you, soliloquist, evade
yourself, that I whose nether-I is one
with facts, who actual in your pending raid
destroyed the thoughtless sympathy you'd won
from loneliness beside an open door.

How irreducible it is to be
an ineluctable fact! To stand alone
for you's to be alone with envy, sick
unto life with that man's life become your own,
though nothing's trivial and all's twice thick
when knocked up by the one one wants to be.

CUSHING

I will not lie and say I grieve
for Cushing crushed between boxcars.
No, it's for my spilled drink I grieve,
for ravaged lungs, these childhood scars,

that breasty Sioux I never made.
With Cushing I drank many a beer.
Some nights we sat up late and made
sad mouths, silly and sincere;

but never such a grievous night
as one with Rexroth and Byron Hunt,
Hiroshima's night, the darkest night
ever to hear two boxcars shunt

from Jeremiah to Kingdom Come.
Sharon moaned in her crib. We wept
in our wine lees. The dawn was come
to report our merit had not kept.

Or if I grieve for Cushing, grieve
for less than him, the smaller man,
for less than daughter or friends, I grieve
for tribes, the body, death, for man.

Besides, I made up Cushing. How
grieve for imagination's proof
of being, which, through death, shows how
life keeps itself alive, aloof?

REVERSE METAMORPHOSIS

One humid night a clanking in the plumbing
woke him up, his head splitting, a numbing
drip from his side as foully the drainpipe burst
and out he fell a man, once roach well versed
in pantry raids, on an unwilling host
who takes him not as Kasper Hauser's most
newfangled avatar, but burglar or worse.
Anxiety desensitized the curse
yet left the anesthetic there intact,
antagonist for torpor to enact—
what new professions, whether of faith or toil!
and what new guilt extortionate of recoil!
This is merely a gloss, a soured footnote
on rotting apples in his eye and throat.

PROSE PARABLES

Performance by a Melancholy Bassoonist

The truth about Sisyphus is much more disagreeable than reports indicate. His ceaseless routine, up and down, up and down the hill, is the sort of thing to which a man, particularly such a comic sinner as Sisyphus, can easily grow accustomed. Laborers know. So did Don Juan.

Every once in awhile, exactly when he never is told, how often he cannot figure out, how possible is beyond us all, but every so often Sisyphus is flabbergasted to feel the stone wrench forcibly out of his hands and roll uphill by its own volition and contrary to gravitational law.

He is not even given time to meditate on this phenomenon. Were he to assume one of the physical postures of thought — the pose of Rodin's Thinker, say, or a lotus — he would be crushed by the stone's tonnage on its downhill flight.

This is the real punishment of Sisyphus.

More Honest than Iago

All very well to call Honest Iago the Very Devil, but given the simple-mindedness of that hoary handkerchief con, do we not thereby slight the evil we have an obligation to find in ourselves?

Othello had his sense of rhythm: recurrence every so often must recur, including love, jealousy, violence. Desdemona was, I suppose, short, fat, inescapably blonde.

All the elements of an honest bourgeois idyll!

Assuredly the evil was in their poet. In his bedrock, faulted, reposed the potential of slippage, and even from under the most domesticated cataclysm, once the great subterranean Stonehenges had churned up, an imp was bound to show his face around some slimy slab, a snicker.

Such are our adversities when black and white are inside out.

Windflowers have blown away the paschal lamb. He sails, front knees tucked under chin, clear above roads and clouds. On earth the virgins, dressed in lilies, are strolling in the meadows. Between these two events hangs the face, almost gone now, reduced to a single eyelid suffering from a cinder, the smile it lavished on the lamb, and one tear shed for the virgins.

"Whose face is it?" The virgins interrupt their twittering to pose this question, then become immediately aware that they are pregnant.

"I don't know," one answers, delivering a baby boy, "but it's been there since sunrise."

Doves, doves!

INCREDIBLE ACTIVITIES IN THE EYRIE

I can't remember when that whoosh of wings
fanned over me and snatched me through the skies
high to this pinnacle of granite and ice,
so stunned I was by mercy that denies.

To fend off cold I've found me a milkless breast
for nuzzling against, and, once I learn to think
in eagle, nestlings for romps along the ledge.
Surely I'll grow accustomed to the stink.

As for the fare, I've eaten better and worse
down home, nor am I forced to read and write
nor puzzle out responsibilities.
Of course, I worry over my trial flight.

But I am rearing hackles where they count
and daily improve my status as a guest,
though I have wondered: could this eyrie be
not an eagle's but a buzzard's nest?

And will the despot of this poem let
me live it out, whatever my habitation?
I doubt it, since his purpose here's to learn
his private death through my annihilation.

The trial impends! Fledglings along the ledge
line up, flutter, and score the croaking air.
Can I refuse the leap? I shrink, fight shy!
Who pushes? How absolute I am, and bare!

JUST ANOTHER APOTHEOSIS

for Sanders Russell

Just why I picked so wretched a morn
to climb Old Baldy I'll never know.
Dank was frozen to the rock.
My shadow, sprite that clove me in two
and who was snugly loath to go
(and why not, since I permitted no rest
and made it hustle even in dreams),
clambered along through mist, a mist
that seemed to issue from my thought
about my thought. Up I scrambled
slapdash through scree, scampered along
ridges in rapid-fire spurts
till finally my breath came short,
handholds mealy and shallower,
and there I clung, cleaving to sheer.
Then mist, clearing in the sharp air,
still hung in swirls, parted, combined,
invading where my thought returned
and turned upon dissolving sense.
Astonied, when least expected, I
sidesaw my shadow outrageously leap
from top to bottom of the cliff,
discharge itself from bottom to top
and caper there, grotesque but grave
between the wall and—what? the sun?
Even the rainbow danced! And I
in hot astonish standing still!
Hallelujah! Joy to the world!

TIGHT-ROPE CONSTRUCTION SURROUNDED
BY A THOUSAND SONNETS

For her to whom the thousand stares below
are one face only, bellowing for her fall,
act is facile, scarcely an act at all,
merely a cross across her will to know.
From ear to ear the farting engine drives
a cycle's neon fenders. On her flanks
thousands of squirming men have broken ranks
to safeguard this moment: here she survives.
Her eyes are patching rope a dozen places.
Intensive balance is irrelevant:
fibre snaps behind her, but she can't
believe it. Were the one face divers faces
she'd drop, her cry analyzed by a shriek,
drop mind without end, frozen in technique.

THE ULTIMATE POEM

The poem perfect through its parts and in its whole —
    for that we long as travelers for home
and homebodies for rough seas. It is not heaven-sent.
    It bides in the exact coincidence
of right feeling and intellect, of beatitude,
    proportion in a signifying tune.
Care is the efficient cause, by which the change
    is brought about. Care's the virtue that weighs
love and perfection, perfection and love, to give them scope.
    One night a poet wrote the perfect poem.
    It's said that looking on the divine face
blinds the onlooker, or scorches him, or suffocates.
    The man who reads the perfect poem will die.
Excess of light? I don't know how; I must surmise:
    his nerves would splutter and blow out, flesh
would flash and fuse, and then his heart would disconnect.
Only the poet, who couldn't read the poem, survived it.
    For many years he lived, tilling, writing,
learning to fellow his solitude. And then he read it.
    When perfect sunrise found him he was dead.

ROSE IN ICE

As when relentless Jack the Ripper
saves Beautiful Belinda Blinks,
or as the fridge preserves the prune,
or both ensanguine through their chinks,

flight is no longer privileged
this rose. It occupies a space
of water stultified by cold,
rigid in an assassin's embrace,

and now, when most opaque, most filled
with itself, is also most concise,
transparent, doubled in lightning and sleep,
a body of flame in a mind of ice.

INSTRUCTIONS TO ANY PAINTER FOR A
"CORONATION OF INÉS DE CASTRO"

for Gabriel Seidler

(Note: Inés, mistress of the Portuguese Infante, Dom Pedro, and lady-in-waiting
to his wife, Constanza, was murdered by his political enemies. Upon succeeding
to the throne in 1357, Pedro had the murderers tortured and slain, and
exhumed Inés, whom he had crowned in state at Coimbra.)

Look to your muscle, look to your heart,
painter, for only travail will raise her:
yours and, over your shoulder, Pedro's,
for she in all was his creation;
and though he divined the answer, the question
was whether to carry his labors further
than any Pygmalion would have dared,
and create her alive when spirit's gone.
But if you're now in mindful sort
to bear Inés, you'll have to forge
her lover too, for separate
they can't be thought or painted whole,
while whole they must be if at all,
despite one seventh of our world
run stagnant in her veins.
                              A certain
anxiousness in handling Inés
will accrue if Pedro's portrayed first,
giving to your strokes that queerness
the subject begs compassion lend.
Concentrate his reach of hubris
into a single eye's tourbillion;
hold him somewhat left of center,
well in foreground, turned to her
at an angle that shows the lone eye only
and gives us chiefly his back, the feature

Constanza knew him by best. Display
your meticulous concinnity
in details of vesture, if you wish
(I take it he has doffed his mourning
and though severe he's yet a king
and not averse to your displays);
but keep the beholder's vision fresh
for bold portent, emergencies.
And that's what she must do — emerge
from smoky shadows coped with, scooped
from smoky light.
                              Across the gap
of the vertical middle axis throned,
right of center in middleground
facing us roundly, her forward pull
must meet his backward push until
we're warned of canvas overcharged
with strain's potential rip dead-center.
Leave that core for last.
                              Meanwhile, Inés
should feel no concentration of mass
around her: yellows and greens best float
and white be final rinsings of salt.
Though dissolute, it's flesh you see,
not the bones, oh not the bones
quite yet!
                              Her webbed gold hair's intact
in charnel growth. (Only later
did Napoleon's grenadiers
hack it off.) Parmigianino
would have found her heron-neck
pat to his mannerist technique
and torqued it like a coiled spring

222

readied to strike. Don't you err so.
Forbear till the seduction abates.
Though flesh be weak, her neck is strong
and stately. Here is where your mass
might well accumulate without loss,
seeing how narrowly move the ambits.
Was it the starling of her heart
into her mouth so blackened her lips?
Yes or no, your black must hurt
us wanly to knowledge of her heart,
not only when it beat beside
her paladin, or stopped her breath,
but now when, failing to understand
how pride could quarantine his love,
her love is suffered as isolate:
for can't she pass right through his flesh
and yet not touch him? Still, he's touched:
her black, no more than she, is death;
his white, no more than he, is breath.

You might avoid the bishop's fuss
by sitting her already crowned.
But scruples urge that you include
one grandee swearing his fealty
on her withered hand. I'd make the bastard
sweat stretching to reach it! Daub him low
in the right-hand corner, the discord
turning a triangle lopsided.
What you figure to left of Pedro
is of small moment: blazons will do,
shadow serve, or the bishop's back
in slapdash flight.
                Now let's return
to where reality's navel burns

for bitter devotion — to the center.
The world came flying, much a bat,
and the bat vanished, much a world;
but at the axis whence it flew
between the fixed prince and his charmer,
it caught its vision to a force
past flying, where the so-much air
postured after form. That place,
best unpainted, could resolve
whatever tension holds the world
precariously in rot: time's mould
can't damage nothing. Yes, to salve
your conscience, leave the bodkin bare.
Finally, an open casement
(above that center, as deep in space
as in history) admits a crush
of fuchsias fleshy in their reds
and purples. Paint them lacking leaves
to show what follows on fatal loves.
You will, of course, be discontent
with partial rousing-to-life. Reward
yourself by painting your own hands
closing the shutter against what's there.

III

THE SINGING

A crossroads, dusty, vigilant
under the sun's weapon, a vast plain
with a solitary tamarind
asleep in remote fulvous haze
far from where the meeting roads
guard the encounters of a sphynx.

All day under the sullen sun
I squat, face to face with her smile,
waiting for the fatal question
that never comes. The tree fades.
Tight-lipped we stare until Orion
passes above the Southern Cross.

That was when the song began.
It spread like gasoline afire.
Did it pour from the winged creature
hunching there? Or from the suture
of silence to silence, stone with stone
and obdurate ignorance of fate?

I watched those lips that never moved
while dawn compelled its vortices.
It lasted while my mind went deaf.
You carry the old place to the new,
it sang, *whereas the whence has changed.*
It is I screaming against the road.

THE DOLLMAKER

Under contract to the church he carves
saints out of wood. His bloody Sebastians,
stooped St. Christophers, and breastless, rapt
Eulalias, discharge pent energies
and forward confrontations to his art,
while maybe a saint will lend him a third hand.
Yet pleasing bishops and the clubbable ladies
is nothing to the dazzle on children's faces.

He never was prompted by an artist's pride,
beyond the fit occasions of his craft,
to challenge, sleeving most of the aces, God
at His own game, as Parmigianino once
in his portentous *Conversion of St. Paul*
where the master's miracle of a horse
sweeps us away from the miracle in the clouds.
In small towns sleeping, children rest the houses.

Though he himself select the wood, aware
of its rugged source, and through devoted days
whittle the figure free, then from his row
of colors pick his Judas yellows, blacks,
vermilion, Lady blue, though he foreknow
the image as he learned to know his children,
once his wondertoken is consecrate
he kneels to worship what his craft has fashioned.

The same wisdom he brings to children and craft
tells how between each doll and a child's joy
a second cause can intervene, his own,
or one that might suspend both joy and doll
(still as a long white wall on a long white day)
while idols of confirmation are enshrined.
Next week I'm likely to be pleased by these lines,
as you, I devoutly hope, enjoy them now.

228

SLAUGHTERING THE COW

A cow so massive, so hilly, it was a massacre!
From the wrong side of a pink-primed wall, well from above,
down to an unkempt meadow adjoining a shanty-maze,
I watch the ritual slaughter from all the isolation
and possible non-being grotesque in a Howard Hughes.
Well, not the slaughter itself: for that I climbed too late.
I missed the throat slit neatly, the huge bulkhead sledged down
to knees and voluminous side, black bellow churning sludge.
What I watch is the ritual dismemberment.
A hedge of over thirty men, women, and children
I see, a dazed burro, mongrels, a shying horse,
a silent circle round the shambles and the shaman's
broadcast blade. First he slashed off her head,
brains jutting. Sliced-out horns are left to puddle the ground,
dishonored. Shouting breaks out. The charmed circle breaks.
Wives (not daughters) rush with buckets to catch the gouts
that spurt from scores of fountains. Redhanded the butcher
splashes barefoot, hideously holy in carnage.
(Brueghel is Brueghel because he owned no telescope.)
After flaying, stomachs ripped out give up the ghosts
of one morning glory and a mess of knotgrass.
Then, offal heeled aside, her heart is tenderly
withdrawn, separately tabled with organs, tripe,
chunks unheard of, unrecognizable purples, reds, greys.
A scamp clamps lunar luck to his skull, those sun-exalting
outraged horns, and exorcises screeching girls
to the field's edge. Machetes and cleavers gash great slabs
from sides, haunches, shoulders, belly, steaming handfuls
whisked away for only starvation knows what feasts,
yet nothing lost, nothing under the bullringed sun
lost, no rumination, no victual, no breath, no value

lost, except one fragment, always one piece lost.
I blink; I widen eyes to take in the circle reformed,
women stumbling with cans of water, sexual knives
tossed to the grass. Without a prayer, or not my prayer,
firewater makes the rounds, a swilled oblation round
and round, girdling the women sowing the skin with salt,
and on the third their globed mouths void water and fire
smack on the skin. Smokes from bristling fires coalesce.
Apis, broiled and devoured for strength, will reappear
in children, all except for that one piece of flesh,
the dewiest, fumiest lump that falls behind the wall.
Tomorrow is the wedding. I have been invited.
But I'm reluctant to see that cow brought back to life.

STORM

Is ripeness all and what's in the howling storm?

When Mother Malaria off the simmering river
cradled me down in her heats and witched me slung
in a dizzy hammock, oh sweetness and light to the friend
who shut me in with jackfruit first, though rusty, warty,
though fulsomely misshapen, though hugely unpromising,
a whelp that only its tree and its mother could love.

But what will tell it us ripe for eating?

He rabbit-nosed the weather: "Wait for it to tell.
Neither late nor too soon it tells." Just wait.
Stable to their complicity, I probed no more,
but settled back to patience, possible loss.
I was three-quarters defunct when thoroughfares of lightning
began to fork. Out of the jungle it broke,
wresting poinciana down to mire. While forest odors
trespassed through the shanty, leasing
an inch (no more) of breathing space, I swung and swung
over and back, out beyond near nothing,
nearer death, nearer life, and fully awake.

By morning, even that bare inch had disappeared,
stifled out, a ripe green air, ripe red,
ripe confectionery fragrance strained back walls
to the thin, near-breaking shell, as braced as leaves
of a sensitive plant, shaking there
in the fever of me, of my delirium
where a monstrous tree with a swarm and a crush of pulpy breasts

danced a merciless morning round my hammock
and whirled me winding deep to the womb of wind.

With my finger I poked the fruit,
one short hour past ripeness,
and found it rotten to its howling storm.

ROSEAPPLES AND NUDES

My blinds drawn down against siesta heat
and Ribera's climax poems unread
across my lap (through shadow they entreat),
here's to outside my hut, distributed
among the bathers jubilant in the stream
and roseapples more fragrant than their namesakes.

The sun that deviously glows my skin,
intimating me in an orb of sweat,
comprehends the bathers as they spin
gold froth from breasts and water scorchingly met,
or dances where roseapples bob and gleam
as ripple after ripple overtakes —

luminous aroma, niveous white,
and deep but simply come venereal red,
both soft, both warm, as round the colors light
revolves, trammels a shout and bridal-bed
of surfaces that pressure what they seem.
Inside, in shadow, odor consumes, and aches.

Whereas the bathers grab for moidore suns,
the fruit commands red galaxies in me.
It wrings me motionless while inkling runs
in heat to drop me sopping with memory,
jungle poems unread, flung to that dream
of roses and apples by Minnesota lakes.

From SEPARATION

3

A yellow, hurt light shivering over New York
now at any hour of parting, infection
pervading towers while the Joneses shun
the Cohens and Columbo rides O'Rourke —
that's how I see the city as I gaze
from jungle towns, who used to glimpse a vision
of how a completing order could be won
that now I see no more. I fail to raise
my spirits when the lovers I love retract
their suasive question (to which no answer exists)
and think it wise to nullify a pact
it took them years to frame, as though the tears
that fall are not their own sad amorists
and every one the face that perseveres.

WITH A MACHETE ACROSS MY KNEES

Yeats had his Sato's sword, a true blade dipped
in stately blood, and with it slashed at soul or duped
our minds with war and with love, at both autocracies adept.

I've got my workaday machete: man-
ufacture Guatemalan, baptized in swear of men.
The scabbard, Indian craftsmanship, is rude; but legerdemain

has tasseled earth-plain ochre, purple, red
in a scheme with plaited thongs, tin moons and studs that, proud
and simple, nothing but scratchwork, shames the aristocratic charade.

Its blade is thick and heavy, nicked but keen,
exquisitely suited for the slaying of sugarcane
or carving jungles up to let us through as best we can.

No less than swords it serves to emblem will,
though chiefly mine is hung to decorate a wall.
A soul in natural function, beauty useful as a wheel:

these I would safeguard, and render them the praise
that sundering denies. Yet it can start a rose
of blood at neck or groin, or heart, should ever need arise.

TWELFTH NIGHT, GIFT HORSES, AND
OF CERTAIN REVERSALS

What we have done to celebrate
our ancient customs, now that they fall
under our own hands, must give us pause.
Most often, little but dry-lipped fear
authenticates our deputized rite;
we fashion a thin forsaking to fill
this green knight, brittle in his boughs,
who should be bedded down with fire.

Fear and its surrogates now tell
what love only is gifted to say:
how we deplete the natural groves
whose fastnesses re-echoed with gods
at play and work. Thereby a tale
of ravage hangs, for winds can't sough
nor freshen till a seed reprieves
a world ill-gotten in its goods.

Even the smoke of sacrifice
creeps like mercury near the ground.
The clogged pores of the athanor
proscribe the wedding of green to red.
Spirits, abandoning bodies, confess
contamination evergreened
and not to be disposed of, for
we roar with fires that rage in the head.

AENEAS UNDERGROUND

"tu Marcellus eris . . ."
— *Aenead* VI, 883

It is not easy for an eye to see
Anchises and Aeneas pacing that plain
in Hades: a dead man bright with what will be;
a live one dim with his destiny and pain,
enacting there, where no man own the land,
what was beforehand working in his soul —
for seeds, prophetic in the earth, expand
and sprout into his ear: "My son, condole
my loss when you are intermittent breath,
not now while give and take with wounds agree
and you your own descendants must become,
preserving fate alive inside its death."
It is not epic for a man to see
his scions slaughtered in a Brooklyn slum.

ADAM IN EXTREMIS

God tackled and pistol-whipped me till I wept.
That was a dream. It lasted while I slept
under my rib throughout my gendering stones
and ended in a clout. I woke with crones
cawing "Father! Husband!", from their assuage
stonecold comfort in mouldering, angry age:
silence, and smoke above the shocks of dead
drift on the city, a hand inscribes the dread
accenti d'ira out of an awestruck head, —
speech, and a telephone booth erupts in blazing
gats and riddled foreheads, after the hazing
the pileup at the goal a ritual dazing . . .
No son of mine shall eat of this rotting flesh;
let them devour my spirit, young and fresh
despite my crutch and salt. This was no dream.
God pistol-whipped me till I had no seam.

GOD VICTIMIZED

There Are Crimes and Crimes

At noon the man was buggered and mugged downtown.
God is his name.
            He wasn't doing so well:
a downhill trade had snowballed into ruin;
Wisdom, his spouse, had left him for Jill or Bill.

Now his name is mud.
            Pants down round ankles,
he staggers up Broadway, Market, and Canal,
teaching urbanites a few more wrinkles'
worth of despair and ceremony.
            Meanwhile
the mugger, ten bucks richer, beggared of God,
our common fate, too strenuously woos
the dread Exterminating Angel's sword
to earn the right to love him and be wise.

God Gone Mad

Not anger, not expulsion, flood, but with a slow
fury of recognition bonding them with Him
in cold heaven and over towns in ripe decay.
And I am they: God and ourselves have come undone
in suicidal truth lacking a way. Who gives
the monk his hole, the hound its moon, harpies their claws,
while God, His brain drilled neatly, bedlamite, rages
and comes at last to take himself for one of Us?

TAKING STOCK OF LOT

Escaping through a hole I've peered in time
I ponder an enigma lit by the glare
from burning cities: Lot and his daughters climb
past rocks, their destination anywhere
away from life on ancient terms, while rain
that shortly will put out the conflagration
already melts the salt imago. Pain
has not completely smeared its irrelation
across his face, for he no less than she
is little more than made her harken back
(although not to's impossibility),
no more than the surprise aslant her face
now melting, and in his own an older trace
of loss, and anciently in mine my lack.

THE BURIED TALENTS

– Matthew XXV, 14-30

We settle deep in this our second mine
and hear the servants harvesting their haste,
      stunning earth and moon.
    Though shaken by a trampling host,
we dream our sepulture's true regimen,

wherein are bared no gifts of usury;
we rest unseeded in a soil that failed
      no man nor, God, not Thee,
    Who might have long since bought this field
were all of appetite accountancy —

until a rip in nature, the roar of which
never was heard till now, to man's despair
      discovers us to his reach
    once more to course the veins of the poor,
once more to clog the bowels of the rich.

AZAZEL

He thrives on deserts: his hands are stones, his tongue a thistle;
water he changes to sand, and a golden salamander
forges its strength in his lungs. His lair is a mirage:
the instant evening fires are lit he pitches his tent
beyond their pales, strikes it before sleepers awake
to flee him, his abominations, where he runs
upon the desert rims, his blur of naked legs
low-lying smoke along a thorn-fired horizon,
tracks erased by simoons that dog him like erosion:
there he estranges kindred with inflation of space.
His solitude's the heat of the yolk of an egg no bird
or reptile brooded, egg begetting itself on itself
in limekiln rites of fornication and self-denial:
there he defiles that incubation with howls.
His temple is a whirlwind gathered close about him
and on outlandish altars suns have bled to night:
there he is not seen in that shrine of absolutes
wherein he claws a rock into his image. (O
dweller within the pales, you must not visualize
those features, neither grave them on your granite cliffs
nor cause the blind to see without restoring their sight!)
His commerce is with fears of peoples who inhabit
outskirts of inner deserts. His eyes and ears are gates
thronged into the dead cities of salt and bronze
where camels are lost in the imagined needle's eye:
the dust of distance under eyelids makes him blind;
and you could take his light and break it across your knee.
Though deaf, he hears, though blind, he sees, like Love, though Love's
self-contradiction, alienation, and paradox.
A sound much louder than his heart, the stutter of hooves
and jingling of bells, approaches; from far-off dizzily

meandering nearer, a shape, a goat, an unthroned spirit
that dreams with the sun in its eyes, piled high and loaded down,
on shaggy legs approaches. Pariahs bite its ankles.
And even the ages rising from behind a dune
are not more laden or gravid with futurity.
Its chin is bearded, ribcage meager, swayback hairless.
He ululates to lure the kite-feast from its freight
of pickled viands, wine, used condoms, moneybags,
silks, rouged idols, Damascus steel, high tablets of law,
war engines, mansions, towers, frankincense, and myrrh.
Into the mirage of whirlwinds disappear all things
that kept the deserts from encroaching on our lives.

THE 151st PSALM

If every second squandered while I sat
unable to stretch a hand or lift a hair
in horror, now together were heaped, and that
more than enough availing to my care,
perhaps I'd never cease, but revel in time
for changing fashions, toys and gaudy lust
and even, Lord, for Thee, Who in my prime
hast moved me somewhat merely since I must.
Of colds that waste a man in Thine own sun,
so that his shadow runs deprived of heart,
and though the going's easy, will not start
a quiet till his perturbation's done
and new contingency becomes the oldest,
the desert's, once its night controls, is coldest.

IV

FIRST LAST WILL & TESTAMENT

I, the poet Robert Stock,
never one to build in rock,
tongue ill-used in such great speech
as sets death well out of reach,
having crept to forty-eight
rings run around my treeless fate,
forty-some dissolved in air
till who can guess what ghost walks there,
sensing in the dusk a chill,
think at last to make my will.

I, who pay a hard-won rent,
can bequeath no monument,
finished or in embryo,
worthy of the debts I owe.
Still, restoring what I've spent,
I'll fend me from a cold descent.
To my wife's prerogative
what remains for love to give?
All's between us, crucially spared,
casually stored, equally shared:
thus, as my life, my bare bequest
pends on Harriette's behest.
To my eldest, Sharon, I
leave what most must satisfy,
she herself, out of whose bone
increment confers her own.
All I have of what she is
rallies to swell her synthesis.
Christopher comes next in line.
Perseverance, large design,

purposive determination —
lacking these, intimidation
all his life must plague him, so
Kit's allotment is to know
resolution's relevance.
Jonathan needs temperance.
For his share may he decline
shadow-battles that were mine,
all the drink I never drank,
dope I never shot or sank,
temptresses that I denied,
rank excesses never tried.
Hereby down·on Deirdre call
pride in great things, not in small:
Beauty, not mere prettiness;
poetry, not prose or less;
love, not lust; and plenitude,
not bacillus of a mood.
Into Julian's care impart
what I am or know of art.
Of my children he's most blessed
with the unremitting quest
that we call the artist's curse.
Should the flickering of my verse
guide him to some splendid blaze,
art will exculpate my days.

Mostly I've drawn this legacy
for a stock that favors me
in little save improvidence.
Let me bestow intransigence
(high-flown buzzard fed on rot),
hope (sustained on what is not),
and, to rinse the loathesome taste,

bringing water to the waste
of blessings glittering above
their heads like glories, all my love.

Codicil

Vices, being volatile,
merit only codicil.
For buffoons to history shorn,
fascists, communists, my scorn,
while to others of ill will,
such as own or dip in till,
my possessions, for the use
guarantees their self-abuse.
Item: to the hater, hate;
item: to the tyrant, state.
No finale caps this list:
items confound in findless mist.

But, stripped bare of means to give,
once again I start to live,
start to gather suitable stores,
raise an altar out of doors,
who, because I for my sake
nothing in creation take,
taken am by Robert Stock,
able now to build in rock.

From

COVENANTS

(1967)

"Behold, I send you forth as sheep
in the midst of wolves: be ye therefore
wise as serpents, and harmless as doves."
— *St. Matthew* 10:16

Though I leave them little else,
this book I leave to Harriette
& the stalwart 5

I

SITTING FOR A SELF-PORTRAIT

Fast friends, the best friends to my ease,
  keep dragging me mirrors, all sizes, all shapes,
  yet much like those of my enemies;
  but fast or loose, my mind soon scrapes
their quickened backs quite bare. Almost gaily
I'm cockled to no face at all, death looms so daily.

Before some bronze Etruscan disc
  incised with toiling Herakles
  or Marsyas flayed alive, I risk
  the spectacle my jaundice sees
(as when in deforming miratoriums
I wreak on style the drygoods of emporiums)

to find that all my Robertness
  hugs me no whit closer than
  reflections on a glass possess
  virtue to seize the glaze they span.
Although pure German; it no longer irks
that women take my face for a Persian's or a Turk's.

Half a man and half a beast,
  the double nature of my wrong
  rapes the bride at her wedding feast
  by dint of my innocent wedding song.
Depending on the angle of refraction,
how dire a man betrays how fell a beast to faction.

The best self-portrait seems to be
  lost at will but found askance,
  much less in ruminating me
  than following my disappearance
into a centaur's disappointed day's
dared night where, forthright out of nowhere, nightmare neighs.

PAUL KLEE

for Byron Hunt

No wonder we exclaim: How like a child!
He hazards wisdom where beginnings are.
By runic stone or skeleton beguiled,

he pondered on heroic growth exiled
to fractions — indistinct if he stand far.
No wonder we exclaim: How like a child,

this wishing us near and simply reconciled!
How like a man, punctilio of bazaar
by runic stone and skeleton beguiled

beyond tamed Europe, deeper than what's wild,
and yet would seem (as paint might trust a star)
no wonder. We exclaim: How like a child,

how beautiful the hand, the heart how mild,
that, taught by blue-chalked wall or bubbling tar,
by runic stone or skeleton, beguiled

an inlier shape of bird, a witch reviled
through calling deeps that closed and left no scar.
No wonder we exclaim: How like a child
by runic stone or skeleton beguiled.

ON A GIFT OF LEAVES FROM DOVE
COTTAGE CLOSE, GRASMERE

for Eileen Wilson

The seasons, in teaching the years to fly,
have taught them well since Wordsworth's eye
deciphered the branches that testify
        these mine, each leaf,
though daffodil and linnet lie
        past grove or grief.

I muse on William and Dorothy,
and through their building vision see
unsettled debts of yew, a glee
        of sycamores
that leave their cascading canopy
        by opening doors,

the builder oak, the white-stemmed birch,
the lichened, minster-pillared beech
acknowledged through time's latest breach
        or closing gap,
and glamoured rowan whose throstles church
        in a berried lap.

Communicant though sere mementos
of nature active without repose:
they may be, pasted on cardboard, prose
        that's merely sensed;
but in the mind that through them blows
        are reverenced.

BALLADE TO BE READ IN THE MEDICI GARDENS

One understands your sort of sun, Piero,
faint, frail, deprivative, a tyranny
to make the sibilants of melting snow
outsing the hammered strokes of artistry,
of the possible the impossibility.
One's skin records your perishing overhead:
an ice-age in the mortal hoarding bred
this *cire perdue*, an Icarus cajoled
into a clay retort, cramped wings unspread.
Oh, Adam's father flies in the face of the cold!

Dark seizures grope in Michelangelo
for cupolas to explode in prophecy.
How can he bathe his forehead in the snow
if ice be warmer to the touch than he?
Despising an art that helps the Medici
like Flemish burghers to weep till comforted,
up from abysms he drags his marble instead,
the very flaws being organs to behold
the soul restored into its sleepless bed.
Oh, Adam's father flies in the face of the cold!

Those starred white flakes that soundlessly must go
berserk in his *terribilità's* churning sea,
those feathery edges clouding the lines of flow,
transform the garden's trim mortality,
and after forty years a memory
of marble chipped in vain, an inchoate head
estranging space and never quieted
will storm his hand, and marble veins unfold

how he from where his David slept had fled.
Oh, Adam's father flies in the face of the cold!

Snowprince, your order got with child by dread
remains, apart in a sunless dawn. The dead
survive the wilting of your marigold
while shapes of snow endure where they have bled.
Oh, Adam's father flies in the face of the cold!

THE HOSTAGE

for David Galler

If Plato, haunted by an eternal past
in which the statue and the law were one,
had laid tomorrow by the heels in a glass,
what rot would he have smelled out on the sun?

Apollo, who toyed with Plato's Parthenon,
was not warmth informing what returned
each harvest to each frost, unless an un-
derground and winestained mystery had burned

that sun in its pitch tides, conceiving time
as eternal now, released from longspun laws
that bind beauty to beauty spared but tame.
Six lions sleep in sunlight's coldest pause.

I saw one beast from six directions rush
upon a fixed and instantaneous centre,
that centre love. Talons in golden flesh
unraveled the design of their tormentor.

Plato in his glass returned my stare.
I knew how I was cast on a wall, flat
to him, but also know those lions were
in his sight round, bright yellow, and newly fat.

THE EVANGELISTS

His mangy buttocks levered high
a stone's throw from some kapoks, the cur
worries a carrion with his foul breath.
A gorgeous oleander and
the sun, broiler of choicer meats,
advance their warmth, but disregard
the carrion — black, indifferent.

Inflamed with hunger and humor, an eye
sticks to the buzzards like a burr.
These dance a stink of life round death;
so debonair, their saraband
accosts their gloomy lord at meat.
He lends brief chase, maintains his guard;
they dance off, mock-panicked, elegant.

While one bird lures him farther than nigh,
a second snatches the carcass. A blur
of wings follows into the sweet breath
of kapok, prizing the trick in hand.
Then passionate silence huddles the meat.
Snarling below, his dog's day marred,
stupidity fumbles discontent.

Let me rejoice with such as fly
(yet, that atrocious grace can stir
humor to craws crammed chock with death
— since my own fare, far from bland,
hungers for shadow more than meat —
hoists these birds by my mind's petard)
and with the rheumy eye lament.

PANTOUM ON SOME LINES FROM CAMÕES

No mar tanta tormenta e tanto dano!
Tantas vezes a morte apercebida!
Na terra tanta guerra, tanto engano,
Tanta necessidade aborrecida!

So many storms and so much havoc and,
indulged by towering Death, such jeopardy
sure-footed on Saint Brandon's spectral strand,
impose their importunity on the lee

disposing that our hubris be unmanned.
Death so many times perceived at sea
stirs up waves that endlessly expand
till being also claims complicity;

but contravening deaths by reprimand,
made booty aboard, Death discards as debris.
Such warfare, such duplicity on land,
we squatters lack our deeds of obsequy:

where wings were, dark fowl screech us contraband
and dayspring's quenched in flushed frigidity.
How, cribbed to pygmy, may one understand
so much burdensome necessity?

So many storms and so much havoc and
Death so many times perceived at sea!
Such warfare, such duplicity on land!
So much burdensome necessity!

PORTRAIT OF GERTRUDE STEIN

1. LIFTING SINKING HEART

and lifting belly fond of a fond a sweet:
for lifting a sinking heart, wine's fat fine.
Is wartime anytime to be in heat?

Fondly lifted a sin unstitches a pleat
or plots an ought we to wine the troops to dine
and lifting belly fond of a fond a sweet?

Composing anticipation and yes a treat
in time saves smocks for soaking up the Rhine:
is wartime anytime to be in heat?

As the house firm and keeps her fondness neat
sinking into or featherbed or moonshine
and, lifting, belly. Fond of a fond, a sweet

feathers boards; then favor no buck to greet
with a shock clocks nor treat yet time to brine.
Is wartime any time? To be in heat

(your fine unpleated fondly stitched, as meet)
sinking heart will cross the border line
while others hem their way. You're a stein
and lifting belly fond. Of a fond a sweet
is (wartime, anytime) to be in heat.

Don't say no to a lady.
Praise Gertrude.

Fourth of July orations
burst charcoal stars
around her head.
She would have said so.
She would.
She did.

Would this fair young notwithstanding
who wants to know: *Is Sinking Heart*
any kin to Lifting Belly at all, at all?
I ask you, would she,
would you . . . ?
Notwithstanding coral lips
and sitting well possessed,
her heart will sink
before her belly rises.
And if our Gertrude saw the ships go down,
all hands perishing,
don't say no.
Did she see imperiling rocks?
Yes, she glared.
Gert rued them,
more than likely even made a note.
Was she for warning seamen?
Yes, her warning
was of sirens
in those environs.
                    We weren't there
but don't say no
and don't blow
bubbles in foul air.

Pragmatic as that or platinum knitting-needles
to deliver *La Gloire*. Precisely she commits her mind
and leads a knowing with a saying to the altar's word.

This other — independent
dependent on conundrums — call her anything:
Don't you find it comforting not to mention fascinating that
*   heresies may without exception be catalogued under E for En-*
*   thusiasm?*
Go to, rub your lips in honey!
But don't say no to Gertrude.
I would as lief
believe a cow could fly as she would tell a lie.
Liefer.
So don't be rude.
She tells time,
she provides us with useful recipes
in briefer than anytime.
Praise Gertrude.

But O SweetMotherofGod to get a rise
out of anything, this other
whose name is nameless:
Don't you find it uplifting not to mention comforting that William
*   James predicted a nogood end for the shiftless folk of the torrid*
*   zone?*
and even unto this day is that prescription
sufficient to the Standard Oil thereof.
And anyway, who uplifted Willie?
Don't you find it dialectically stimulating not to mention ambi-
*   sexdrous to conjecture on whether or no the sirens treated the*
*   boys to "If You Knew Susie"?*

Go to, rub your lips in money!

Should she say so,
don't say no.
She warned us of war
circumventing the orator
and ending up where it was before.
Her enthusiasm
was never subject to schism:
she glared: she was strong:
she bore Willie along
and told us with her moxy
the evils of folksy
factory orthodoxy.
Did she give birth to knitting-needles?
Did she believe in knitting bones with figs?
Don't be lewd.

Don't say no, no.
Praise Gertrude.

3. MALCITADO

Lo! her guerdon
as lovely as falls the chance meeting in garden
of a rose and a rose.

4. ONE IN AMÉRIQUE

She would have made one an immaculate doctor delivering al-
most as many babies as Dr. Williams or peremptorily one a
scientist undiscovering irresponsible process or a ruminant tres-
passing in the public gardens and daintily stepping over toadstool
and trillium alike or possibly pentecostal under a bigtop or just
about anything that is something much (as more than bridge-
builders must be both) but above all a filibuster circumstanced

away up in gertrude heaven/Inasmuch as she knew what she was
saying while and before she was saying it, how could there be
continuing assault, squalor, miscomprehension? Not from that
throne putative, compulsive, normative, while she was telling
what she knew by doing how — proceeding, overtaking what is
abuilding, letting them confirm her one and accordingly more
substantial and unexposed than they who were indeed no one/
She would have made one a most immaculate and subtle doctor:
Merrill Moore and Murillo Mendes are not in it, certainly no
clinic chief is in it, almost as many babies as William Carlos
Williams, and most inventive who was not to be stopped, still less
her discourse/To thread perpetuity

MAGNESIUM SUNDAY

in

a perseverence of: cut it clean, severely, continuing in joy:
breathing in and out, the dancers in and out of one another's
arms, in and out the shore and sea/Wherefore she invented many
one in giving them to give all the cost, the pent up cost of her
interruption, ear, and it endured from the beginning before
which there was nothing like it to an end after which there can
be little about nothing; for many were one supremely in her be-
ing one before there were many because she knew what she was
saying while she was telling what she knows.

5. PANEGYRIK UPON GERTRUDE

She propertied in words an intimate prize
no other, set in Eden to canonize,
dared ever disengage and charge with light
deduced from the sole source of that word's right
to point its trait apart from entities
compounding only toward the inbred frieze.
Nor can they anymore Saintsbury her measures
than syntax could bear witness to her pleasures.
Hers the covenants of artifice,

269

hers the pure mimesis as accomplice:
to understand and to communicate
were one resolve; in all, her perspectives plait
into caressed particularities
unsmirched in critics' inkwells, unrivaled by devotees.
Don't you find it flagrantly excessive not to mention de mauvais
ton *that Crates, ugly wrinkled cynic of Thebes, should con-
summate his marriage to Hipparchia before an indiscrimination
of spectators?*
Come off it! Many, say a skulk of foxes,
say a cowardice of curs, cursed poxes
on Gertrude's happening exaltation of larks;
while others, much enlarged for matriarchs,
crept into couvade to tingle them warm
Parcourir à loisir ses magnifiques formes.
So, in the nature of things, she trusted scruple: fire
answered to the purity of her desire.
But was she an ought, demure when she nursed groans?
Not likely! Better; she gave them credit. Her tones,
tough, chided the apes lumbering through strait-zeal
that of its mother hoped to make a meal,
or railed against the well-greased arbiter
from Michigan to Spain betraying her.
Such stolen pangs will deeply dig their pock
no less than meteorites avouch for shock
marking archaic calamities of the clock.
She sensed the bloodbond sworn — that was enough.
Now miles that hitch and hike us up the bluff
that she conceived are blazed by hamlets of one.
And if we hovel, palaces are begun
on ridges where the stones turn into wheat,
and though we spring her wine, not summer's heat
will strip her weathered vineyards of the cool and sweet.

THAT THE SESTINA IS WHAT IT IS
DESPITE WHAT IT IS NOT

Knowing what even scholars have surmised,
that through the sestina's synergy there thinks
an always felt symbolic mystery,
I laud its ritual, and celebrate
whenever spirit, circling among six words,
leaves a sesame for the devil's escape.

The devil and scholars, dullards of escape
under lids gone narrow, have surmised
this punctual dance a mathematic of words,
Anangke's free verse in which he thinks
to maim free poets as they celebrate
unsheathings towards a central mystery.

Because, blind seers, your stony mystery
can soar in an eagle, think not you escape
the Sisyphus you nourished. Celebrate
freedom affirmed, triumphant beyond the surmised,
uphold the angel feathered as he thinks.
Yet freedom, like subjection, will, in words,

rant only of rims. The serpent's still small words
are deeds: poised to round the mystery
with its own tail, refusing when it thinks
back Christ in meekness renouncing all escape
from bloody incarnation, the serpent surmised
how golden is the feast we celebrate.

There is little cause to celebrate
the stonehenge eagles drop around our words:
upon the serpent's refusal, as poets surmised,
a present but undisclosed mystery
of trinity recurs. When townsmen escape
into the Devourer which the devil thinks,

remember: the devil only thinks he thinks.
Swollen gowns have lean cause to celebrate
what fate would call a glorious escape
into an unliable tyranny of words.
Orpheus, who compassed mystery,
enjoyed reserves hell never had surmised.

The point of refusal thinks no limit on words.
We celebrate the threefold mystery
in no escape the heart had not surmised.

TRANSFIGURATION: NATURA NATURANS

I, one day abashed
by my voice breaking

on its one stabbing string,
ashamed of my mouth, a twisted

tide-stranded starfish,
of this grotesque body,

awkward, without presence,
on its own bones crucified,

of hair like a bramble
and knees like a jackknife,

I, *mirabili dictu*, I
even Thou transfigured,

this whole of me
(by one's indifference

befouled as any star
in a wayside ditch)

transfigured, wondrously surfed
by littlest graze or loitering glance.

AND YOU, TOO, BRUTUS

Behold this beggar, traitor, thief,
a scandal to his kindred clay,
Esau & Ishmael past belief,
this stuprator who wrests his prey
        from temples of grief.

Of his father's substance prodigal,
he strips his worth to lice & bone;
but fearful of too far a fall,
drags an easy guile back home;
        intolerable

in stench & sloth, sly fang & greed,
to beast & brother, foe & friend.
Though maps be plain, he will mislead;
though true-tried bolts your door defend,
        behold him succeed.

In time he burns his father's thatch
which is restored to him in faith.
He beds a freak — she's bound to hatch
an adorable child. Is it that fate
        has met her match?

Yet — such his luck! — he swaggers free.
His morrows brim with him, though empty.
This jackal, stoat, fox, buzzard, ape
(whose mother's hope conceived her rape)
        holds every key

impending in his privileged grip.
A natural nexus, the times' upstart,
he spins a rope of sand for a whip;
bullets ricochet off his heart
        in fellowship.

He sows the deluge and crops sweet corn,
his arrow unerringly drives to its quarry.
Some claim that he's a scapegrace born,
but others that to the greater glory
    of God he's sworn.

The routes are dark where his disgrace
forbids our righteousness to follow,
so dark we cannot fathom his face,
too bright the eyes for us to fellow
    this goat of grace.

Until stayed sanctities have spoken,
how should one know or take the token
that riddles his forehead? Will the last
man seal the first man's prospects, past
    all breaking broken?

Fleeing the poisoned town, they met
him loitering by the well, his hand
an arrogance on the parapet.
The elders of his native land
    provide a chaplet

of gillies braided with swart hellebore
for one who cast the die for garments
his crowned & murthered brother wore.
They garnish him in sumptuous vestments,
    tempt him to whore

wives & daughters, make of his sty
a mansion, fattening him to die
the day he plumps his natural span.
I would be afraid of this man
    were he not I.

TO TUI: NOT TO HIE HERSELF OFF
TO ONLY GOD KNOWS HOW DIRE & PESTILENTIAL
A SOUTH SEA ISLAND, BUT TO COME WITH US
TO FOUND HER COMMUNITY IN BRAZIL;
TOGETHER WITH SOME PREPOSTEROUS NOTES
TOWARD AN ORNITHOMANCY
OF LOVINGKINDNESS.

1

Don't sail, Tui, where krait and coconut-crab
bitter are, embattled to work you havoc,
and where appalling shapes, alert, dim-herded,
rouse in swarming shudders from spume-combed cells
to wrap your battered selves in polyp shrouds.
Coral is cruel, that never cordials hurt heels.
Christen your boat "The Coffin" — it's Charon's craft
and naps you where grey rot is Robinson Crusoe.

2

But rather, I implore you, Tui, come
and hospice our Island of Banana Groves
by the River of the Valley of Parrots. It happens:
all at once the covenant is ours
to bend where light invades our prismed choice.
Nurture due the day has been accomplished —
fruits and flowers gathered, greens and grains,
turtle eggs collected, breadfruit baked,
shoots set, boughs lopped, fishing spears and nets
put away or drying, jungle propped back
as far as need be, but its vital resilience
clearly more pressing than ours, no farther; and we
redeemed are, met in qualitative coign.
Then, tranquil by the river, cream-thickened

278

and purple-blinded in its fugue of mirrors,
in scent of frangipani, touch of plush,
we view the unexploded sunset's fuse
through hyaline coils of an emerald treesnake,
the world's most exquisite emblem of paradise.

Jackson — on the veranda bent to his verses,
the cantor of love at the georgics of our year,
the white face still, remotely phosphorescent,
the black beard trailing among hibiscus — makes
a study for Martin Buber, Marc Chagall
or Max (with antelopes in Brazil) Jacob.
Lovers fumble in Brooklyn; their inner bones
half humanize a factory when they kiss;
while Betty, near us on the bank as real,
goes tinder to an old love's antennae
no lliana can swerve, sun drug nor ocean deepen.
Jaguars brushing her flanks, heraldic, Jean
glides from orchards where golden-hived cacao,
beestung under moist leaves, candied her mood,
and flows untouched into the tapestry
her subtle stride of self-possession weaves.
Ahda, like the compassionate shepherdess
in *Daphnis and Chloe*, hands an Indian brave
through bosky coverts: amplitude of rivers
unreels an anaconda to fathom the twist
of her roots' fanned anchorage, her kelson of wings.
Their hands sticky with star-apples and mangoes,
our essence-temporalizing children prove
motmots not alone among the birds
that through this sundown decorate their beauty.
A pool creams, merry with churning, and Harriette
with hair and skin vibrating like an eyelid

is born of it, Harriette of shoaling thighs,
and even shells cry joy, and ripples, joy!
and my heart with love swells vaster than all Brazil.

                    3

Red feather sickled into a macaw's wing
is somnolence before the gloom draws down
and closes up the oriels of the leaves.
Sole song to eastwall sombre back cascades,
holds the pulpy sky to ripe interregnum,
one beck of ecstasy keeps perched the hooked beak.
Puma and prickly pig suspend their skirmish
to hear love shaped in the irapurú's
brown throat.
                    The rufous herbivorous loose-dangled wolf
lopes up; fish leap from pink unruffled foil,
like hummingbirds poise midair; and sloths,
fungaceous balls that budge for nothing short of
famine and toppling trees, bark their shins
scraping down, come rub-a-dub sidle and dusty;
the piume fly has reared himself a throne
on the carnivorous flower's gorgeous rim;
and shrub-aback caymen come waddling round
playing host to orchids and parakeets.
The lordly jaguar sports a toucan crown.
All garter branches sagging with butterflies.
Nothing flutters by, all stays, all stills,
then yields towards the blood's sung undertow
amassing torrential fêtes, unbinding floods
to fling across the spell on thresholds, binding
changing present to the changing past
in which, feathered and fathered, song first issued

torn and bleeding from too meager a throat.
This is where they are the most themselves,
where they have never heard God's nervous tread
tormenting narrow cloisters among the trees.
Blue Dragon, Vermilion Bird, Black Tortoise, White Tiger:
this is where they covenant with peace.
Yet none below discern him (no more Sebastian
numbered the arrows), aware though they must be
that this the throat must thrill for them to dwell
splendid in the chimed prisms of self-grace,
as the intolerant saint be riddled for peace
to reign.   He seems to sit him neither on limb
nor nest: the trunk's too tall, the dimming crest
too dense, bromelia-choked; but he is axis
between a groundbreaking star and the charmed circle
soundless in a standstill dance, a far clasp,
his carol presented to each, each separate note
an equal end, continuous redemption.

4

Only the bellbird, shrilling its taste of zinc,
comes to church to mock. The macaw shuffles
along its perch; butterflies turn to moths;
—I knew a garimpeiro claimed it's luck
against the crotchety blood's anabasis
to carry the miracle's feathers in your pocket.
Don't look! the jaguar has devoured its crown!
I smell an eternity of Jerichoes.
The ground beneath the tree-pole, splattered with blood
and starlight, now infertile, murders the tree.
"Here," our fables will read, "the meteor dropped

that taught us how to wrest our right to the stars."
Hacked shell, red talon and claw, scorching breath.

Under the slope we kindle fires. Vanilla
gorges our lungs. A tapir's blunt splashing
unmoors the widening trust of nenuphars.
Do palm trees suckle the Southern Cross with dew?
All day the moon, all day was wraith, demanding
hands like candelabra to uplift her
palely from among the scourging vines
and recusant hands that drag down passionflowers.
As deluge of remembered song recedes,
leaving all the world a shore, we find
Sebastian's corpse behind the oleanders,
the tiny fly disgorged by the timorous bloom,
those blood libations in the heart's deep troughs
that defy reality with reality.
Don't sail, Tui. All the world's a shore.
Make haste slowly: the butterfly rides a snail;
the bearded infant rides with bridle and spur:
Achilles, knowing the wager, loses the race.
Make haste slowly to annihilate
the web of concentric deaths that muddled the river,
slowly to pierce the cirque of heed and song;
for, bald and brown on the shore, the irapurú
makes prose of the sun as, peace subsumed, he retrieves
and concentrates the wholeness of the day
to stream an aisle to the moon's concentric seed.
But on her shield splayed, what screed amazes
the pigeon falling through eternity
to end up smashed against a factory wall.

STUDY OF A HOUSE WITH GARDEN ATTACHED

Her will to come on one Greek, archaic, nearly
overwhelms her repose. But except for nostrils
like the entasis of a Doric column
and indisputably a cornucopic dispensation
from Aphrodyte Kallipygos, she's not
archaic, not nearly. Equally striking's her desire
to seem concurrently papist and Frau Sorge,
towards which end she dry-havocs Pascal
and ruminates on the Abbess of Port Royal.
Precisely what her tactics at the poet-rending
might have proved is susceptible of gloss,
not by reference to any experience
unenjoyed if not to tedium denied.

Among her maids, who serve meringues and a wine
pressed from the pseudo-fruit of cashews (but Nilce
has black eyes made of quixabas, coaxing shoulders
and a sweetening mouth that probes by divination),
Dona Isaura converses in seven tongues
(but Nilce pressed my tongue between her lips),
nevertheless must occupy appointed
imperium: decadent martyrdom, misère
well tempered by cushioned south. Ichnolithic,
inspissated in ceremonial smokes
of smiles that smoulder through deliquescent gums,
her mystical finger signs startle the doze
of winged requiems in bulging brocades.
Her boudoir's bedizened in cerise and cerule
like a mandrill's bottom; from her balcony

delighted eyes bisected in cusps of quatrefoil
mortgage Cupid's blessing on her amours.

Senhora, your attractions (on alcohol
stems uprearing a pose of your blue rose)
excite curiosity but hardly concupiscence.
Greek alkahest! rococo tropical!
Senhora, after leaving you, I pitch my prospects
in your garden, patchouli, jaguar's-paw
and sumptuous canna all in a bloodblown row;
by seawall burdened under wind-knotting
white dawns of vanilla (before which prowling pulse
walls flare and reel loose cataracts of lime)
I lurk, and each as I brush by
nuzzles against my cheek's slope
like the moist disturbing lips of Nilce
kissed behind the kitchen door — her lips,
yes! same savor, wine and browsed anise —
naked shoulders tendril-nibbled — breasts
two full seas bruising my headland — same
thrush-soft laughter on tiptoe, so recklessly small
stretching up and so prolonged to my backworlds —
and we lean into the tumid noise Anonas make
bedding down against their inner rinds.

THE POET MÁRIO FAUSTINO DESCENDS INTO HADES AND RISES TO THE EMPYREAN

I. DAYS & YEARS

Pummeling the winds it came, spoiling for a brawl,
came only to fly foul of an Andean wall.

Testament no trust, no verticals of light
to the crazed condor, though it purr like a dove
at speeds not even Mário could love.
Be no satellite to death forged in an arrogance of metal.
Immense and dark the bird went beaking through the Andes,
dispatching its cargo of discord, trembling and tenderness,
its genius and its genus that no wrinkles will devour.
Too fragile, too crazy in its fragility, it came
clutching to *The Man and His Hour.*

Pummeling the winds it came, spoiling for a brawl,
came only to fly foul of an Andean wall.

Nineteen hundred and sixty-two.
Today is nineteen hundred sixty-five.
We have broken, today, the neck of space.
And only today, this nineteen hundred sixty-fifth,
am I struck down by word of the disaster that smashed a word
no dictionary could define,
the verb Mário wrecked where suns of the Brazils decline.

Pummeling the winds it came, spoiling for a brawl,
came only to fly foul of an Andean wall.

Three years, years through which the things I said, did, lived,
if not a lie, were somehow incomplete,

fragmented, unreal: behind the stack of unread novels
a few raisins whining in their mould;
abundant life I thought smelled of white bread hot from the oven
is by his death conceded scarlet fever in a darkened room;
my journeys all begun but never ended.
This nineteen sixty-fifth I localize
a vagrant melancholy, a vague unrest, a tale untold
that tells my vistas Andean, bleak, bone-cold.

Pummeling the winds it came, spoiling for a brawl,
came only to fly foul of an Andean wall.

Nineteen hundred and sixty-two —
nineteen sixty-five —
and inbetween how many left to rot from my side!
Most lime's not quick enough; slowly it accretes, expands:
one by one the great ones die, the rogues, the gulls remain.
Time's bursals ache with all the caskets it must bear.
In '63, in Dallas, a death that in the balance
of truth and essence
weighs far less than, Mário, yours, yours sudden,
compelled me to the worrying-wall. But that ill tide
ebbs now, Mário, since I know we did not share it.
Let the rogues and gulls continue to devour it.

II. THE CONFRONTATIONS

The death-spark, black on a grey weal, breaks
bleakly, bone-cold in the void it wakes.

Andean corridors twist and turn
towards a minotaur that is not poetry,
unknown but for its cold rewards
of buttress, gendarme, pitch and gorge,

of sheer wall raging against sheer fall.
At sunrise and sunset there are gules
emblazoned on the *disjecta membra*
of stone-old convulsion, churn
and counter-churn; times between,
the minotaur that is not poetry
beds down in grey; peak-islanding cloud or vapor
thickens to rock — cold, silent, minatory.
With massive intent, the glacier presses on.
The battlements, grey-folded inquisitors,
assemble to pass sentence on space.
First to die is the horizon.
Is it as dark in the minotaur's belly
as here at the dayspring? Thereupon,
infinity, and then eternity, contracts,
dies. The headstones, borrowing time to pay paul,
perorate without inscription or grace.
Last to die is time itself.

The death-spark, black on a grey weal, breaks
bleakly, bone-cold in the void it wakes.

Born, Mário, under the mango's languid shadow's
dream of its fruit, the rose and green and yellow stains
recurring on your face, your body's bones in concert
with the hammock's harmonies, you were as now I see you, now.
Mid-afternoon. Silence, saturated with yellow,
awaits the hour of jubilation. Red-tiled roofs
extend their circle's pleasure,
and beyond the river, the jungle and sea
rondure their perfect bubble always on the shores
of bursting into iridescence. Crystal globes of resin
exuding from the mangoes . . . hummingbird's hover
reshaping hibiscus corollas . . . . In striped pyjamas

you sweat through a poem's labyrinthine measure
into the paraphrases of the bull.
Shoulders (cupped to capture the myriad scents)
and oily beads (brilliant on your forehead)
counteravail your sexton sense of briefness
that turns and twists into the Judas month's
most murderous day until, at the core poised,
all the world as language becomes transparent treasure.

But the death-spark, black on a grey weal, breaks
bleakly, bone-cold in the void it wakes.

III. THE FALL

Always he veered too near the sun.
While Icarus, still melting, falls and falls,
Mário's fall has just begun.
Slowly the void empties and fills.

The bird's *disjecta membra* falls apart
silenced in the glass that totals the greying of hair.
Separately they fall, the things,
they float down separately.
In smokeless chimneys, the fuselage, an emptying valise
(what vulnerable chockstones!) clog; and smoking debris
litters the ledges of the heart.
The jetstream's hung one leaping instant in the air.

Always he veered too near the sun.
While Icarus, still melting, falls and falls,
Mário's fall has just begun.
Slowly the void empties and fills.

How many, Mário, years! — how many do you sound the air,
leaving tux and striped pyjamas far behind?

Too fast, too fast you hurtle into gravity's garments.
All over the sky the stars are falling. Snare
the sky, it's falling! But Lucifer, who falls apart
forever and a hazard's day-by-day,
dooms the heavens back to their crack of care.
Were waves quite years, you in the sapphire millennium
would have bathed till doomsday; but,
death knows a shortcut:
you ventured wing on the abstract wave of air
only to be mutilated on the metaphor-without-a-poem.
And yet, too fast, oh Mário, too fast,
you put your changes on too fast.
Pervading the whirlwind, you change its course.
You pass the giddy samphire-gatherers.
You pass, vertigo of the ages' slow upheaval;
you, your body like a foetus curved, you,
fleshing the kernel of the transilient void, you,
lover to the end, encircling space with your arms.
You falling blur my eyes. Oh, climbing toward your face,
my fingers freeze to the handle of the ice-axe.
Is there some peak you do not dare betray?
Are you in hiding, absconded, from those who love you?
Mário? Are you trying to tell us something?
Mário-Lucifer, what are you trying to say?

Always he veered too near the sun.
While Icarus, still melting, falls and falls,
Mário's fall has just begun.
Slowly the void empties and fills.

IV. ANTI-PRESENCE

Your unicorn is in its blazon sealed.
Impossible to bear you from the field,
impossible on your Andean shield.

It was a touching thing, your body. Like any other body,
touching and touched. It felt itself at home
on featherbed or cactus. Home impossibly
was where the body touched. But rocks? But lost on rocks?
Oh, Mário, Mário, while we paced and talked
morning into Lorca, noon into Crane,
and kept our talking earnest while the other poets
slept away their youth — the rocks, did the rocks
already lie in wait just beyond the jungle heritage
you learned, a child, to fear? Or did they only then
begin to form, stalactite to stalagmite
conspiring in the mental cave? We talked an age
a minute. Now, am I to suppose that you in your shoes
as old as Adam when he gave the name of quartz to quartz
met your death on something older than yourself?
Today, at some odd angle, a rock once red with you
goes black with terrible remembrance. No!
I too am rock on which your blood goes black.
No! You'd just as soon have lost a thumb.
But all that touching. Lost? On rocks? Lost on rocks.
Impossible to bear you from the field.

Impossible in the void to find your body.
You have outgrown your body.
Spilt on rocks, defiled by birds,
you have outgrown your body;
preserved in ice
where fingernails and hair
still grow, you have outgrown
your body; rarified
and breathed like a sacrament
in Russia, China and These States,
you have outgrown your body;
or, a scruple of earth

affording a bird-dropped seed
its cradle for the root
that bursts the mountainside,
you have outgrown your body.

Impossible to bear you from the field,
O serpent in your blazon sealed,
impossible on your Andean shield.

V. PRESENCE IN HADES

Mário, plunge! Plunge to body's desire,
you who ached for little save to string the lyre.

How could the lances of the legions of rock
impede your plunge through earth
since you concentrate them all
to your breast? As Icarus by water,
you by earth are drunk, you vanish below,
head, torso, ankles lost to me.
For I am not so wholly spirit-born-of-pain.
A rock, indeed a grain of sand, can stop
my eyes from reconnoitering the Hades road.
First my libations of grief must flow
to mollify the harsh ground. Then, eyes rinsed,
soul clarified, I see you once again,
see you descending and drinking Lethe dry,
know by your smile you still recall
latent syllables that grappled with your earliest poem.
Though Charon, in deference to your right of tenure,
refused his pay, it makes no difference, none—
right through the gold *cruzeiros* you see,
your eyes are fed on everything except horizon.
Anointed, garlanded by Rhadamanthus, you stroll

in the calm shade of a grove of laurel and mango trees,
O poet, and discover Virgil and Sophocles,
Mallarmé and Pindar, Yeats and Valéry,
and nuzzling at their feet, alert, the minotaur
who drinks their words as yesterday he drank your blood.

But when the nightingale draws
her burbling to a close
on the third of her four falling notes,
leaving all unsaid,
and inexplicably from the swallow
leap capriccios, you,
Mário, inexplicable Brazilian singer,
feel the pain resurging to your breast.
Surely there's another realm
whose song concludes unforced,
where the dead prolong their dying
(without rude contravention)
into the pure instant.

Mário, rise! Rise to soul's desire,
who for so little ached except to string the lyre.

VI. THE ASCENT

The true bread, Mário, will rise, a full loaf,
the leavening in the sacrament —
oh, not in time, but so his wafered body rising
meets his falling body dropped amid the wreckage
in a geological and a prayer's age.
And they will smile at himself and shout:
Welcome! Welcome to the Delectable Mountains!
And having given himself back to himself,
having nothing (except his genius) to confess,

intact he'll hover over his poetry, a hummingbird
reshaping corollas, unseen but resplendent
in the blue haze of death — the same as always, the same!
And nothing will have changed, though all is different,
though something will have civilized our wilderness.
His death was a green grape, sour to his few years,
but his own sun is turning it purple and sweet
to our understanding. And, as always, I will cavil:
"No, no! My God, Mário! Not this, not that, not the other!"
Or, simply: "Yes! Yes! Yes! Yes!"

VII. THE SIEGE OF LIGHT ON LIGHT

How the air sustains you now!
The waked void slowly fills.
One and by one
horizon to infinity
perspectives are restored
buoyantly, diaphanously.
See: the tangled underwoods
now sheer line, pure scintillation,
light! And line itself dissolved
in its own consummation. Oh, champaigns of light,
lilies and birds of light, laughter of light!
your eyes and mouth a total radiance of light!
Secret, essential crystalline,
perfection of the light sole element.
How the air sustains you, luminous! now!
Yes! Yes! Yes!
Luminous now!

THE IRRITATED OFFICE

(after Carlos Drummond de Andrade)

I want to write a sonnet stonier
than any poet ever dared to write,
I want to paint a sonnet that is dark,
dry, strangled, impossible to read.

I want my sonnet not to arouse
the least pleasure in anyone,
that in its malignant immaturity
it will at the same time be and not be.

This, my antipathetic impure word,
must punish, inflict suffering,
a hangnail under pedicure.

Nobody will remember it: a shot in the wall,
hound dog pissing in chaos, while Arcturus,
that clear enigma, permits itself to be surprised.

THE SYNAPSE

A paternity suit was brought at ten o'clock
by the pretty twenty-eight-hundred-year-old
            brunette, Erato,
      against the impecunious poet,
            Robert Stock.
            Need I say
she flashed a leg and won at a walkaway?

Just after lunch, in nearby Hippocrene,
Polyhymnia, stately his wife and thorn,
            haled him to court
      for impotence and failure to stork.
            A veiled queen
            who chose her drudge,
she towers, pointing him out to the priestly judge.

Meanwhile, from garret to alley, from the Groves
of Academe to the sweet Castalian springs,
            he chases a bitch,
      his cockscomb mustaches a bristle
            unto her alcoves:
            though plagued by laughter,
it's the unlovely Clio he skitters after.

Blear-eyed, foregone loaded on song or beer
or God, he wakes to the spent bouquet of sex,
            and, temporal sequence
      reasserted, counts his blessings:
            the chandelier
            draped with a black
silk stocking, all his members out of whack.

But Clio's vanished—gone with her passionate cries.
Her stocking rots before my pried, propped eyes.

III

REVELATION ACCORDING TO THE BELOVED

My love on Monday rising fair of face
will glide like a white ship on a wide water,
for she so tenderly is amazement's daughter
her wake must pity the spirit of the place.
My love on Tuesday rising full of grace
will dance like the moon candidly with the sun
to end in luck what was in luck begun
since she with nature keeps such perfect pace.

Then all night long she'll burn her day's carnation
across dark sheets of sliding water, burn
so bodilessly bright and finely drawn
into her lover's arms that revelation
will grace him carelessly, and he will learn
to meet the dawn as whitely as the dawn.

MARY ON THE DEATH OF JOACHIM

In memoriam, Floyd McKinley Stock: 1898-1957

In clear March wind, some weeks before he died,
my father pruned the pear trees, and he spoke
of how a sweet and wholesome yield would pride
our hunger. We knew, after his side's pain broke,
we'd take delight in the fruit without him. Shrewd
yet rich in my mother's mouth, that savor's sake
will stay the love they bore much fortitude
in one another. Once I could partake
of both; but now, tears are shapen pears
which to my mother taste of their pledged kiss
beneath the arch, that tenderness toward prayers
that generated me in original bliss.
Drop, white blossom, never mind the May,
achieve full fruit for ever yet a day.

THE SIXTH STATION

for Harold Holden

Pass me through, Beloved, as light through glass,
but stain me, too, with tinctures earth delivers
to plead the prism-love Thy Way uncovers;
thus blazon vistas where my soul-comings pass.
In my longing's dark of ages panes of color
glow, gloom, and glow, beaded amber, and crimson,
angelus amethyst: the proffered woman
glows, white sun being bridegroom to her dolor.

Gloved in quiet, Veronica suffered the crowd
with a veil unveiling Grace, the Son in a cloud,
and flamed me all color's after-constellation.
        Thou eternal O eternally Thou,
may I too brave their fury; Creator, allow
me the veil and stain of Thy configuration.

THE BANQUET

The late hour, fattened with horn and tabor,
    presented me the cup;
but cautioned I must drink it up
before that luck befall my neighbor.

While yet I pondered, a creeping stain
    cumbered the cup, the drink.
Our absent host had missed that stink
and part of the terror, parcel of pain.

The wine and then my gratitude
    vanished in tumored smoke:
at bottom swarmed a venomous brood;
my fellow guests began to choke.

I bruised the goblet underheel
    and fled into the street,
dreading that somewhere I must meet
my neighbor's bleeding palms, and kneel.

POEM ON HOLY SATURDAY

for Harriette

*"Now also we know the excellence of this pillar which
this glowing flame here lights for the honor of God."*
    —The Blessing of the Easter Candles

"The cistern contains; the fountain overflows."
    —William Blake

1

Tonight when all that flowers, on the air
and in the wide withdrawal of menstrual tides,
dilates our breathings past their magnitudes,
when the expanding organ counterpoints
erect grass and pollenheavy darkness,
the vegetative grail of space comes full.

The shuttle Pacific isolates and plaits
Asia, America here; the vast reveals
vision flowing over our mitred flesh,
binding the foam-starred vigor of our divided
love-atolls into sole continent.
So once a planet was born of the salvaged sea.

2

Somewhere the candle-trinity's inflamed
pillar by pillar, as you are made naked
to sacred hosts in my profane flesh . . . .
    *May the power of the Holy Ghost
    descend into all the Water of this font,
    and make the whole substance of this water
    fruitful for regeneration . . . .*
Tonight, fire enters water and is renewed

303

in rampant pyrosome (O hollow serpent
contracting to your fountain sanguine flame!),
reiterating Jesus erect on Gennesaret:
that veritable light by which the lover
Tristram, of worn rudder and shivered oar,
when *every track was a flash of golden fire,*
taught his quadrant of the seven worlds
poised, of daylight locked in stone of words
until the resurrection of The Word.

3

Constellated as The Crystal Whore
overnorth brain's brothel, Magdalene
seeds, ripens the air in its eunuch year;
winter breaks in groom and bride of flower.
Pressed, the heavens are prodigal of stars
that flare out of extension and are not:
oh, neither in space nor in time is room for us:
we can only enter into each other,
only into flower of bride and groom.

RED CLAY SPEECH

Rather than set her to music, keep her in stone's
rebellion, mute, against rain. For she is not
to eke out the guitar's frail shell.
Return to her some darkness, an ur-light,
jointures pregnant where the bell's mouth choked
that would not urge her nuptials to the clouds,
emerald for that unsubmitted grace
of illumination, and for her mortal heart
black basalt cut in the round, but delicately,
delicately, for also she was hardened,
concentrated and a long while fused
down there, she too outwaited the agate-snail's stare
into the eyed stems of acontías.
Now would you pitch her trembling along some wire
to keep a gaggle of old girls company?
Come mellow, come shrill, she'd be inaudible
in the too exiguous ear's wreathed room.
Keep her drugged in stone: Medusa's head—
also thus will she be held a mirror up to love.

THE BEACON

Dido at wit's end of Dido, your fates dispersed,
you clinker down: your generous bridal-bed,
his effigy, the bronze heaped high, but bled
so etiolated that flames, prolonging their worst,
can't instruct us where the bed's framework burst —
unless it be where sunrise, breaking red
and gusty, kindles its sinews on the roadstead,
unless you rise to labor without thirst
or burning breast.
                Aeneas, higher bound,
lies too liquid to the seething ground,
too reflective stares in the setting sun
to pluck you from the snarl that you have wound
from ends at odds. "Pass, Trojan!" growls the hound
of Hades. Dido, your small fate, just begun,
will burn in Rome till destiny's undone.

ADAM LAY IBOUNDEN

Asleep in space, he labored death on time,
so deeply his own shroud that God's footfall
wavered a weight of winters before its chime
could reassure Him Adam heard His call
and would revive. Then God, His paradigm
all but complete, left the man to crawl
still sleeping into the road of his ribs' grief
and there encounter who would share belief.

Quicker no lightning, a cold moonstorm that burns:
past hillocks green and native to his days
blackening while he looks, past red ravines
coagulating in his eye of eyes,
through chasms cysting to snare him, snarled by vines,
through nettle-sting and parching flux he goes,
nightmare-ridden in nightmare's own countryside,
its parish of the love-inflicted wound.

The beast on his back now gone, the land spreads flat
before him, fig plump, palm salutatory.
Fumbling behind him, across the void just fought,
the beast rides trial of promise to take lost quarry.
Adam lies quiet. But though the brook at his feet
invites, he cannot stir to drink such glory.
He, bounden to the bond, wills not to forsake
those blacklands. Thereupon his eyes awake

and rise to Eve's, cool water in her hand,
her hand upon the lips that marvel her name.
And they begin their travel back through land

so healed he scarcely knows it's where he came
before he calmed to her. And then they stand
before God's face, and, proving in love no shame,
share in a world that rises in His view.
What more can happen to divide these two?

METAMORPHOSIS

That Adam would was from the first implied
by all that was not God: by that embrace
of margin through which forms burst from His face
and moon and cloud and frost elude their guide.
There was in Eden that ripening under stress,
that rendering of his enclosure; with ferns,
with zebra and zodiac in sight, he yearns
to plot the elaboration of consciousness.
That from the apple's sanguine to its core
his teeth would gnash, was gospel from the start.
These planted pips of myth provide a store
of curious growths, yet few such forms bear fruit.
His left side vanishes in chaos; part
of the man remains behind to sound the flute.

MOSES ON PISGAH

I, Raphael, my Lord's intelligencer,
murkiest fume from the wasting of the thorns,
I, sheer radiance sanctioned by the flame
to persevere with Moses to *excelsus*,
I choose to proceed behind this climbing death,
its own self's son needing no solace in sorrow,
no paean since no thicket hides a ram.
Unlikeness greater than rift between two names
flares here; for Moses, be he that which he may
besides the mountain's body, rises in awe
that rock breaks no tablet of its word.
The climb's an upwardness that overtakes him
stonily out of his skin, ordaining him high
on summits where his spirit, with trusts deferred
and desires all but fulfilled, fulfills his counsel.

So, when he gazes down upon his people
— so silent a horde below, their beards pouring
like promised waters over eroded breasts,
their flailing broad-sleeved tumult, horns and timbrels,
their tempest silent on the plain below —
he who strode always inside a ring of flames
and not with kissing roused fate to the tryst
but brought down plagues and clove the reddest waves,
now neither ponders them nor wonders why
he enters Canaan only through his eye.

Distance nearing distance, how still a wait!
How clear a vision of the promised land
is graven on his eyes already stone;
and light, beating upon them, might be rain

on vineyard, fold or temple. What is blood
that he goes stiff when it runs coldly sweet
as water filtering through sandstone years?
Moses, that rock of his people's destiny
through whom our Father cannot pierce regard
except He change it to Himself, could burst
in fragments for time's ice to dissipate;
but lo! the man and I are not alone!
God is here, and also Death is here:
Death, a cipher stirring in the womb
of God-filled space — and the lily breaks our ground.
Who else . . . oh, what else, except that He
Himself should delve the rind of fruitful stone
and with His two right hands bury His dead?

No thunders crack, and still the horde below
see diamond-lightning of the mountain flash
into eternity, searing their eye;
and then consumes to ashes only I,
so angel, see; then turns opaque again,
grosser than before; and seals their sight
from brilliance it will take till dying to find.
How gloriously, how full of grief and grace,
we angels recreate ourselves into
the greater glory of the image of man.

Appendix:

SOME EARLY POEMS

CENOTAPH FOR TWO BUTTERFLIES

I doubt if you'll remember (we were younger then
since bygone time seemed younger far than we)
how we tossed all afternoon, blowzed with sun
in the light of a sky-blue-watered cornfield,
unavowed to white-dusty road and heat-hazed farm,
how two butterflies, one sulphur, one black-barred scarlet,
fumed out of dazed yellow and out of the world.
A cicada spun its wire the hark of splintered ground.
One would swim, such days, with crows, glossy in the noon-open.
And later, while you were buttoning your blouse back up,
one, the black-barred burst of scarlet, reappeared.

I didn't know, then, why it swooped on a sudden,
instantly to purpose, vestigial,
as who should hold you, never having held you, fast.

THE DANCE

Came south, tripped up by constricting manzanita,
south by the red-in-umbrage of madrone trunks
withed by such rankling greens as anguished Grünewald;
came down where cypress, not less adamant than agate,
lower graygreen blackribbed umbrellas over Point Lobos,
taste of seastorm still cumbering late leaves;
by fir cones mouldering in the loam at Big Sur;
swept past opal swelling, fumbling a clot at the core
of sundown, past headlands where seal yelp and plunge;
hitchhiking south to scour out winterings with sunlight;

approaching posterns to Death Valley, guarded and kept
by nipples pectoral-plated with unyielding snows
that, lacking suck, salvage and chalice fire
in bird-abacinating rigors of chipped jade and topaz.
And scurrying south, the cluttered, curdled clouds
high and quick away — swifter than vermilion scythe-wheeled
chariots of Cambyses, fleeter than sallying shadows—
warn us to run, quick and away! high and quick away!
But it is mid-day. What can die upright in the sun?

Then we two stood where old rakehell sun
spends his desert's buff among the multitudes
of sages and sweetclover-tugging sands, an absence
of memorials, and these: Joshua trees!
Trees? warlocks in coveys of contrary force!
Trees! Lot's wife in fibre! lightning-mummied cauls!
gravel-scoured! Behold how gnarled and blistered flanks
rock in the merest breeze-excuse, how verdigrised sarks
tuck high and wide round bristling thighs for the lavolta!
Percussive a crust as the flogged beast staggers in heat,
stint nor let, numbed incoherence beating
floral hints into convulsed loins. Those twigs are claws!

Watch with me; I could not bear the ward alone,
danced under. Better bury than leave exposed
the dead. Better to consume them wholly —
therefore, viaticums of dance. But what if dancers
be themselves mixed bones? Lack quicklime, am rigid:
so firstling solitude treads mercy down a corpse.
Will dancing exhaust the rite? Oh, do not leave me!
Hermitaged with these would soon console corruption.
My eldest-born fought succubi and stood alone
beside an empty tomb, stood stone, believed.

Sun is accomplice to a terror of roving rocks,
Birnam Wood of cinnabar and crumbling ridges
environing green residues that smoulder
the while we watch, burn ochred haze into red.
Have we come thus far only to be beasted thus,
mocked, murdered on the stumbling branches of a dance?
Sweet sun, your phalloi have no part in this,
reassure me!— what device asserts these desert thoughts
that press on me most like Rockies?
                              I left her.

                                        Three days gone
and her body's oils are still acid on my fingertips.
Now should I, as though from slaughter, fresh lave and dry them,
crazed roots, in chill water, hot wind, wands
never again laughed white?

Bah! arms akimbo, knees askew for nimbler leaping
are without flux, phalanxed in measure and profession
petrifact. This desert cauterizes lust,
drains interiors, leaves nothing to the hand
save the lifeline, leaves me cold with my dead
in progress through this murder's cracked rim into red rock.
No, no! not sun, and not accomplished evil
induce this terror, but the perishing mind of green,
mind that can think no thought because a solitude.

Her thighs' clear fountains splashed me with —
but that was under other stars,
nearer thresholds of daffodils.
An everywhere and forward-hunching night
hugs warlocks to a far recessional of mountains.
Anathema, sit! Are they cruciform?
And surmounted by a crown of thorns!
Hood me in eyes that I may see.
I stretched my arms to sanctify my Lord,
extension of my love being His sign:
and my extension sings the upright tree.
Across the wintry posterns, a kraken moon
is decomposing on the salt floor, unrhythmically
humping, collapsing; while, my side death, the great
midnight's pinnacles with their shadow-shoulders cover
trees that offer too many hands too often to wounds.

Green mind, green mind, already almost to the thrall
beyond which nothing green may pass into the heat's
honed inversion (though like in carious death),
though chasm by chasm up you ply, unlike evil good
does not accumulate, the adversary never
wears away, a little sunshine here and there some rain.
All at a bound you gain or hands go begging.
Green mind, self-ordained in meditation to pace
those crags, beware! it yearns, the dead-dance climbs!

But I tonight, haunted, scarce choosing, resolve below:
not in any event to be attending lover
of the last thing in the world
that must at any cockscare cross over into the valley,
and though the red lip crumble, mockery for comfort,
not to wake at dawn crucified by splinters.

VISITATION

Deep-founded bathylites their heavings fault
to spurs, pocks, glares of water, red-rimmed salt;
alb ants rend Jerichos round Pisgah's site;
nitrates glimmer, the river's smothered in silt-
glide series; fissured, flaked are the flutes of gilt
where two prone pillars fold impacted flight.
"Well may he wince from grit-puckered sea-anemones
who seeks his leman. . . These, whose appetite
schemed back to flames, have cracked the last requite
my sleepers tender femoral Symplegades."
Thus Lilith by my pillow. But what give you your groom?
"Ask the salt-tear, my weltering paps. Who knows?"
— or ceases to care? The everyday sense grows
fatal gneiss to apprehend the shapes you assume.

FOR SHARON, AS SOON AS SHE WANTS IT

O my daughter, supple bird on my branch
with visible veins like cobalt rivers
under the tissue of your flesh,

don't listen to their shouting —
they will mislead you
as they would mislead the daisies
had daisies ears instead of golden eyes.

The peace they concede you, here
in this ticklish world you take so kindly to,
is with one hand given and with the other
dispirited away, the taking mean, like shadows
that in a sun of evil, warn your heart
that not in love their hands abide.

The licorice night with flower-cobbled sky,
your spacious right, still undisputed,
to clean ignore the Painted Desert,
that red-throated diver you wondered at,
wild wild snow, furrowed earth, your kittens:
all come over you with their innocence
till you would be as a sparrow following St. Francis
or that gentle ass that journeyed into Egypt.

Yes, every park is gay and brisk with children
(birds, they flit from every cranny and bush)
and those are pretty curl-cymes in the mirror;
but you are not wholly at peace here,
there are images the mirror will not reflect.

They will say to you— congealed grease
sticking to graceless dignity —
that unless you change your ways

you must not, at last, look to them for help;
will clamp down over your laughter
leaden lids of impotence.
That is what their words mean,
drab grey in a dulled sky.
Yet you will up!
Earth will not subdue nor cover delight
such as yours. No,
priest to you
shall be your faith
and shrive you expectantly with each heartbeat.

My dear one, lighter than lilies,
with your two blue iris blowing,
they are right
                and oh so wrong!
for when you find the walnut you clutch
to be bitter, black in the shell,
what is it you do?
Why, shag it away
or set it adventuring in the bathtub.
Well, watch them, the grievous mouths
puckering at the corners, more each day.

I tell you this not to frighten you
who are my daughter,
not to lessen magic you discover
in every stick and curve, in every whirl
of the dancing leafage of your body,
but that you may never submit your strength
into the weakness of their power.

IN TRANSFORMATION OF AN IMAGO

Movement? Weighed down by hails of trumpets and days, what is it?
If she be there and yet be here, embrace pulsation,
participate in a word's throughness, recrossing intervals
between presentatives and the spiritual *antro nympharum*,
and give to motioned need an unpaled garden's hierogram.

For centaurs more than triangles burst relation.

Could I laud you as an ocean lauds a continent
for being immense, mumbling so to mouths of sand
that shuffle endless steps, in such part would I praise,
but anthracite and mummy, night!
and taxed imperiously with orphic impatience of sight.

When Troy was sacked and the heights came toppling,
less than you stood
steadfast in Egypt, only to meet herself
wild-eyed, reviled in a garden, face to face
hymeneal ministrations at a whore's death, hand in hand.

Pallas Athen' was not of your bosom: ideas gross,
midwives moribund, and how a matrimonial
murder adds another name or benefit to loss;
but, wake in a calm, marbled swell, embraced causes
returned her by the abrasive *Poseidon Hippios*.

History is where two any people who have loved
depart appraisingly each from other,
unfurled in the lengthening line of leaving.
Her heart beats up into her eyes
to see the winestained horsetaming prows returning.

And tithe-trodden patience bursts in the nexus of a kiss.

When in octaves of wax and incense we consumed
the Argive doll, the skill that tuned a phorminx
to nightingales spanned cordax across those flames.
Same awe raised walls interred the root:
O trampled towers, ancient swarming underfoot!

You who like the orange flower and fruit at once,
be it written: you are intersection, brant roads
converge upon your near horizon,
convened are trade-routes all in your garden
where unicorns roll in the many arms of a single rose.

THE WANDERING JEW AND THE HEAVENLY HOSTS

1

Resting from faring among those ice-flares, halt birth and the un-
　　projectiled never (O peace) to grapple,
the hero with his visions, Ahasuerus, remembering him how once
　　his tribes' flocked tents had tarried
where trickles honeycombing glossy stonedrift lit vigils for
　　tuberous thirsts:
how emissaries loomed at arrival, bearing boons, wine in wrinkled
　　skins' intolerable silence (rumors: Antiochus slain in
　　Egypt, mortal torch in Lisbon); departed mutely, no
　　bread broken,
while Ahasuerus watched from prospects selfed of exile founded on
　　how, once, they had been eye, lid. Now women glided be-
　　low
muffled in exhalations. One tall liquid woman, trailed by goatish
　　juvenescence, slips out past the tethered asses.
　　Ahasuerus, rust-blurred wild ass, beheld first one return,
　　quacksalver, then the other,
deceiving all his seasonableness by lack of even silver on a quaver;
and, under dawn's allegro, dromedary yesterday's commemoration
　　spread a trophy of trampled tracks;
how that time Ahasuerus would not chaffer anguish off
for quake petty and peregrine,
would not follow after,
but abuts world-extremities, for there is cognizance taken of thrones
　　and altars and kindred skulls displayed in public compass,
for these ratify bells inextricably skeined with underbelly dark-
　　ness, the blue, the blind, the winged mass immovable;
but straddles oceans, giantry marooned in meditation
on the diaspora of archipelagoes of stars whose filaments, crossed
　　and recrossed, throb impulsions of his exile;
but bids their frozen heraldic quadrille to order, concentrates
　　suspended hostilities, their notes.
Night, however, night and the plain cities couch like unkind lovers
　　apart.

2

January's Taurus
pluperfect, who pointed vernal equinox to pasture, drilled the zodiac
        host before sponge, coral and snail could calendar loose
        plunging ooze,
our crossed night's red-eyed bull
still with the Pleiades huddled leach to his wind-embattled shoulder,
sitting still before the single-sealed veronicas eclipsing only the
        baiter
— for what is he totally waiting? Why doesn't he gore
Orion's spilled blue belt and blue-sprawled burn?
Orion who stalks the hare forever startled underfoot
Orion so stalked, beset by so many shrilling fixities at once — see!
        the scorpion upon him rising, rising into his setting,
and, rising, Dan, patriarch among the forced-march fires.

Cataract-reversing harbinger, wild wet irresistable Sirius-thirst
warping pulp abloom until it lifts in great green striving sheets
        reflecting man and man's dream of man, nightmare,
whose hooded eye draws freshets from the narrow-corridored
        foxglove nectaries,
whose jackal droughts come stranding hyacinth bulb and filigreed
        tender-tangled roots of cress and mint,
so I may pledge his sire, rife spotted sun the spoliator, in
        parallel if invisible drafts:
held, though; held so — cataract in suddenly ice, a sponsoring
        image, cicatrizing dreams
paralytic under the indurating lava of awakening.
Better to have slept with kings and counselors in the earth!

Of flights, engagements with the incunabulum of light: O feathers
        falling in flames on vineyard and orchard!
And how it bled us, how the phoenix carol undertook our love, a
        helix bringing me to bear, me and mine the dread bird's desert
        bred and bled, and then
supplicating all Arabia! The dream of man's dream tricking sleep.

325

And thus it falls I riddle out my equal's torque and thrust
on a couch under overwhelming way with roaring leaves and nuptial
        sabers
that strike me across those scarring generations that honeycomb
        my breast.
And warm sands mourn
like a small command in the throes of a vast love.
Dispersions, of destinations!
Flight's hearthstones!
Who carries his father on his shoulders!
But cleaving, O immobile eagle moulting lakes of radiance that clog
        your wings!
And you there, fearless opposition, amends, O Cygnus, leaving
        waterwakes, lavings of milk, mica-flurry in galactic ash
where all your forebears, Eagle, Phoenix, Turtle, plummet.
but oh how cunningly the Cross configures in the Swan!

Now lime into a daynet each cold wind, hurl them deep, deep upon north,
        we'll take this dripping undulation, Draco, yet.
How it eludes! It girds to strangle Herakles, Cepheus, the Bear cub
        strayed,
and when upward, cradled out of the stint, you pride your poise at
        having caught it — loins! concupiscence purring through your
        will
and under you (spinning, spending) the woman
swivelling seed with wound insinuations can unspring your
        ganglion-range.

                Scorpio, scuttle your venom
                through her bitching blood.
                Judge her at last who too long
                called herself Arbiter Virgin,
                whose intact maidenhead
                fleeces mirth from song.
                Waste her with your poison,
                Scorpio, custom her bed.
Shadowless, heatless, virgin gone to sea
on purpose to get her sick with lack of morning,

326

descending hidden rivers from mouth to lower gut,
there stopping, croaking to virgins still outside
how she will turn the lover inside out.
Not she who scopes her mantle star-embered
at epistle-shoulder, Stella Maris, concern
bluegold on the deeps. But Justice devours our past
and skulks from its scions: Virgin, Scale, and Blade.
Look! my own hand forestalls my failure; my flourish
crimsons precept, for sometimes, Aristides,
I bleed on ostrakons for running to read.
And yet, yet grandeur: was this frankpledge tool
subscribed by me as spirit's trothed reward?
For so is evenhanded amplitude
my own, not virtue's dallying her shadow's
extinct chaos. Under her conjunction
whirlabout ardor dwindles to the bard's
paper empire, nevertheless from which
upon us solace, some thrall and ransom bless,
like the mother's ripe solicitude
that palmed a glory round the liable head,
but under her conjunction lacking flesh.
She pares the truth down to a mimic skull,
abstract Cromwell in the rectory.
One instant claps a beggar together, scrapes
his cry through flinty furrows, muscles your arm,
but wounds, perturbs your soul succeeding to fear
of writs, kings, shepherds following the star
Anareta, adrift in the universe,
incurious, mapped, of Anaxagoras,
all fearful in its vortex of violence.

> Scorpio, course your venom
> through her stream, then die.
> Be a funeral wreath
> interred in the sky.

Boötes draws his silence stonier in than bone sucks flesh;
he like a younger son repulsed from a brother's wedding feast
broods apart; one bid to guard a father's dancing bears,

he rankles inward;
when from the milliard issues— mischance, perhaps, the herdsman
        in his bitterness unmindful,
perhaps the hitherto-undisclosed-but-long-awaited bolt whose
        volley fissures collidings of air—
issues Arcturus.
Natals of yesterday-stanched time in sodden linens, clouted-in-
        the-cradle lacerations
score in carotids the crowded keepsake wards
hazarded in night-again journeys, Ishmael to the east of the faces
        of his brethren, Dan in flight and chase
reeling back where lysol in thuribles
swayed for twenty centuries to dissipate the moment's bereavement,
now returns with history's grief palisading the celebrant
until, occasion's pharaoh, red waves stake their claim.

Had fancied Boötes but my kite escaped the day before
tonight fouled up in my planet's threaded maze: a species of
        pact, illumination.
Then angels cracked their whips.
Through telescope and midnight-crouched through conjuration
the spheres came choired, providing me, preparing me,
oh, not so poor a Jew as most would swear, though poor,
and pure although my guardian angel whelps on every altar.

So it is tonight I seek out rogue-errant merchants of Rhodes
        frozen in their golden snow, gorbellies lashed to barrels
        of sarsenet and aromatic footgear,
so I ransack the fleshpots for Lydian whores and sailors from
        the isles, singling out tall caps, short capes,
blows of spiny cramoisy and jaundice flickering where they fall,
all such men as high in the troubled eye of a sail mark with hope
        Arcturus tremble to spill and Pharos dropped below the rim.
"The sum of shorelights lapsed," I tell them, "lapsed,
can only apocatastasis, the home brew, confer you cheer?
Or earth with its falling sickness tied to its single moon?
When they have withered you out as they must on boards, the candles
        pooled at either ear

will stretch you farther along that voyage than, there, those
        lights, or these . . ." and the sweep my arm protests
cannot otherwise than cosset harlots in the rotting grain.

Emblems vary. Gulls combine to pour their crystal floods, trumpet
seven scattered chevrons, on a splintered wing the seventh lagging,
nevertheless upon your lips the dash, the drill of wormwood as
        third gull dives
into bitterly pacing waves.
Great Pan is dead!
Mangroves oh agglutinous in untied fluvial shadows,
the stroke is upon you: splints of flight to race your age off
        ninety miles a second
and what, if love be not creating love beyond the sere exact, are
        forty annuals tolled by light?

Although from where I wander winds withdraw their wars, sailors
        render dark passages unsafe, am valued at a neckblow like
        a hare, and merchants
forward accusations, collusion leaning on their firepots' circles,
provoke new law or reinvoke committed restraints.
(How cunningly the Swan configures in the Cross!)

                    Between the spectral instant
                    — flood-flashed rivers
                    cratering, uncratering —
                    and the hissing Hydra,
                    snarled webs of water
                    commerce. In this process
                    of remorseless coda
                    Corvus, a present hunger,
                    feeds on geniture quarry
                    to keep mortal the temporal
                    synthesis, *auctor aquae*
                    still oozing from the deluge,
                    and, unaware of the river's
                    abiding gestalt with its victim,
                    attempts th' eternal stasis

of which he's but the hunger.
Like case I strode through rain,
unable, for fury pelting
my face, to see the stars
that burned in all my scars,
hissing, spectral, unmoving.

Ciboriums of littoral hibiscus
trammel scarps of phosphorescent lunes
swollen as logs in sudd and salt and time
until wind springs, until a golden shower
vibrates in space like true south, unbinding
ranks to leap and lapse toward where I stand
holding the Centaur's heart in my beating hand.

The process natural, abandonment gradual, proceeding much as
        figs drop, herons soar, residual
at last, at last. A sun to ripen with; and there were children
        gathering the playpretty spoils of streams at pebbletag,
play that ended in the sea where it began,
and other children, varied colors, sundry tongues,
rearing castlewalls and digging moats beside the sea;
and artists, too, that poked in the rubble of warm, mourning sands,
looking for distorting semblables, a woman's thighs or stance.
The sun crumbled, in fixed eyes
pearl and violet decayed, yet left their residue
like ships quarried whole in the alps.
What skittered through the fig trees and seemed to some enough
        of horror
loses entertainment to the worm below.
The final couple gone, someone had forgotten a guitar which
        plucks itself
till sand, coral and sponge drug its half a gale; inertia.
All try, abandoned pebbles, racial ruins, devoluted grotesqueries,
        the voracities of erosion
claiming no kin save Mother Brine and Father Evisceration,
inertia tries with concord's church exposed on my palm
conclusions.

Conclusions of what?

> Field of feldspar red-respiring
> in the cast dawn of my hand's blood,
> Saint Januarius's blood
> quick in a phial once a year;
> or, center without circumference,
> nowhere of everywhere transformed
> into unrepeatable somewheres of love.
> Oh, we'd shout Mar's crimson down,
> in his own bile douse his wick,
> if only this sexual intellect
> were become the pieties of man
> when time comes key to the fatchance
> re-warding vascular green rain.

Who interprets such concessions?

> Restore, but only
> to this instant
> lent

the highly-wrought cenotaphs of others canonical in his counsel:
       Herakles, sometimes master of astronomy,
mercurial Theseus who weighed the arts of husbandry upon the
       buttocks: remember, restore
at least their tillage and course. Curled round the fruit's
       heart the worm sleeps,
the tunnels where for centuries he munched through ice and alp
to reach a few thin planks, perhaps preserved, so nothing might
       be left undone,
no Ararat, erased from his purpose. "Memory is not conserving,"
reminds the philosopher, cities thorned in his heart,
       adiaphorons in his eyes,
"but creative transfiguring."
Ich dare well sain in no charitee
Jammes and Mambres brote in the blighte frogges
but swiche powre not hadde to clere lond agin.
Behold be beholden, cross of our Lord, O flee
all ye contrarie, Jesu, Seint Sebastioun

seeled in your bloudy woundes,
Sagittarius
bless this haus fro eche wighte
fro nites mare. Where wonnest thou
hote, colde, al betweene? Where gottest thou memorie?

       I hold this Centaur whole
       who still holds me,
       this centre in whose cavern
       Sophia (who spilled
       God's light the broads and deeps
       when, rending heaven's membrane,
       she befell epiphany),
       Sanctus Sophia, Maria
       here created Ova paradigm,
       set a cry between her breasts.
       It burned, it burned on the waters
       like a tall ship at high sea.
I remember, I remember tents strewn from river to river across
        a plain.
Like chicken tracks in snow the seething memorabilia
contract toward umbilical seed and worm's precession.
       And when her wisdom wells
       and recoils upon her fullness
       and ticks in every cistern,
       here to the coronal cave
       a second night she will recur
       and as she once prepared her womb
       all night to mine the day's
       tellurgic lust, a golden shower,
       so she (the same cracked mirror
       cracks the wall, hibiscus
       in a vase, the bible open —
       as before — at Apocalypse)
       will halt at the seventh gate
       in the ephemerid of that hovel,
       will flay her of flesh, divorce

the ornamental bone,
   preparing herself for God's embrace.

Somewhere else, somewhere children remember and whimper for pebbles;
      castles are Gothic abominations;
the mistress raves from couch to couch and is not purified;
somewhere else Mary's insurrectionary son is being purged.
There I am overdue. I spangle you, Sagittarius, back among your
      fellows:
remember my face, recreate my puckered hand, transform me, for I
      will return;
but only from the moment.

Since Taurus, cut-down Phrygian bull with scorpion-worried testicles,
Gemini's coal is ash and wouldn't melt a snowflake.
What will the white bull make of the rigid sisters except he ravish
      with insinuation, bind them with their silken speech?
In the blossom's charred mouth no spirits dwell, no warmth in the
      crypt that dreams its state — Joshua's tomb.
Cancer's jellied ghost consumed sky-resilience
yet kept inflexibly to its abstract, multiple system round an invisible
      star.
One of two, a Cancri fell. What could succeed
but, after such truancy of solstice-falling, crawling?
That crater was not seen until, ubiquitous, breast-bastions crumbled
      in its widening arc.
We slept, and from our shallow luminary, sleep, we could not see,
not even in the arc-light flashed across the sky,
how sidelong shadow nibbled pastures bare.
What painstake, merrymake or process in our lives
recast that spacewright copedance
into this obscenity clambering out of the salt-slops?
Those 12,000 sealed out of Issachar's tribe, whither flung?

Into the dark he goes slowly lightless.
Clouds like snow blow lightly round.
Polyphemus burdens his circles. Rings the buoy
at full sea contending. The nature-nomad warms his lichened hands
at lightning. What a cracking up of planes
baffles, buffets, slews the water-stabbed choirs of habitation!

"Eye or, which first darkens,
mind? How firm the sensorium when pain's quicksand grates beneath
        lids
and the spectacle dazzles out in a grinding of colors? Is it hale
to stay violence, summed-up cast-up sunsleet,
to tense it against a war-concentrating mind's cry swung
rigid and unpardoned, ever in blue-lipped weather?"

The savage, having swallowed God, dances and sings: they shot him out
        of heaven.
But Ahasuerus waits, outwhistling stars.
Below him Patmos,
an undiscovered harbor or star on Mary's mantle,
secures a beauty grievous of Arcturus. That was vision on water,
water surrounding vision, a ship afire on water,
Chryse come to grief engulfed,
preserving bones in nacre, blood in nectar everywhere,
protecting under transparent rind the balance
of seven perfect scales, meet as hands and breasts belonging to
        the same body.
No ripple demurs where cloud is kindled from below as from above;
yet three rings at Philae radiating from an ibis
make the perceptible circumference that is the day
when Moses fled to law and Cambyses fell a lawful prey.

Sagittarius he has held, theurgy transforming legend lines
once blazoned sole and orthodox-bridled chart;
relinquished, though, to interpret love set sentinel to love.
Tumbled on his bed of stone, behold a vision's woman, always naked

and smelling of far stars felled, who aims an arrow at the sky.
Tomorrow, maybe, strolling through a copse, will stumble over
       hoof and man
dead, heart dislodged for her indifferent sacrament.
Eye or mind? Distinction here's a secondary diversion: neither
       feel
the ghost striving to make its presence felt in unplanted flesh.
Re-creation or paralysis, Arcturus or terror?

Celebrate Patmos, these few jagged acres where olive roots
are shadows bruised on rock, yet in whose caves and at whose
       stiff-in-peril breasts
Arcturus ripens timelessness.
There, on Patmos, there it shall seek the earth halfway.
And Patmos too must leap to mine the plunge.
And that locus of concussion, is that a seed and your heart
flowering life and bursting hate? Poor Boötes, with never an inch
to call his own unless he pitch his harrowing declensions
into this sparing tithe of conscious earth
to harvest being.

Turn within to inside space, Wanderer, return, prepare.
Old patriarchs have forgotten how to tend their campfires.
Prepare for spring released from apprenticeship
to Calvary and Capitoline steps; prepare,
you are the second messiah summoned.
Always, Ahasuerus, it was up to you, the spring, the thaw,
yours the concern to burn the anthracite that blocks dawn's tomb.
Turn, return, prepare, and consummate. Oh, then how shall the moon
gasp to see her brother's orbit
sweep beneath her feet, stooping to divide
hurt from wound.
Silence follows the leopard, lightning the tiger,
and thaw is instantaneous with miracle.
So that greybeards sighting will exclaim:
           But which is time's initiate
           and which are after the fact?

which world is world and word?
how must I set my watch?
Birds without arena, watches without here to there.
So greybeards on their epicycles sit them down
in memory alone, their vortex of violence shorn
like stripped gears. The single substance prevails.

O loosening, sundering of pressed packs! Wanderer, climb!
O Ahasuerus!
Pass Ezekiel's unfulfilled Jonas now fulfilled,
kenspeckle the seer's visions with the wisdom, strength and
trickeries of your eyes
seeding blind and tumbling furrows. Grip the trembling reed and climb
to where hibiscus in pollen-flurries fall upswirling deeps of the
under-you-nothing centuries,
where all the suppressed voices unfreeze, leap forth like Ephesian
sleepers
and Patmos opens out in the dancing flower of Apocalypse.

— 1952-3

AT AN ABANDONED SHRINE OF SAINT MARY AEGYPTIAN

The wasteland slips and crumbles past the threshold,
      the lintel splinters on the ground.
Inside her niche, a thorn of sunlight pierces
her flaking, dark-fleshed image, crimson-gowned.
Mary, O Mary, do you feel in the dark?

Blessèd, yet sinful one, and broken-hearted,
      inglorious in your own shrine,
where does your hermit stray? Were you forsaken
because you tumbled in the weeds with a swine?
Mary, O Mary, were you alone in the dark?

Your need to seal pilgrimage was boundless:
      so Samson died not a moment too soon;
so Milton's vision glowed in faithful eyesight
to flash the crystal bright at darkest noon.
Mary, O Mary, can you see in the dark?

The ferryman, to raft you across the river,
      exacted you in a wrestling love.
You smiled, disrobed before he'd done demanding,
and ventured him the breastings of a dove.
Mary, O Mary, were you there in the dark?

His punishment, they say, was an agony
      burst blind and flaked by leprosy.
Perhaps. But never by the hand you worship
and not by your mouth's curse or prophecy.
Mary, O Mary, do you call in the dark?

A few half-withered stalks of rosemary
      still lean together in the garden.
Accept a sprig. There's yet some beck of fragrance,
though not enough to beg of you your pardon.
Mary, O Mary, do you hear in the dark?
          Are you here in the dark?

INSCRIPTION FOR A TEMPLE OF CLOACINA

" . . . as I got a rake
And up I fished this delectable treatise."
–Robert Browning

How these must be larded down with im-
pedimenta, overlorded by names
pondered Persias gone, contingent under the deck,
so clinquant a flower
in febrile pink, yet fragile
as when— so murmers rococo to rust — Fragonard a sapling
betook himself to improvise
fitting addenda to fountains
agate-greyed, dim-beheld through willowy motes,
yet abandoned them after all, instead
glancing pink film in. For even as to here
Descartes as peacock fails us not, anonymous blooms
perhaps not autonomous, not to be trusted. Narcissus
is persistent guest, an' Guv'ner Duff 'mums.
I fear, too, Sibrandus Schafnaburgenesis.

Should I name them after all, subvert primordials
when my cloth is to divine a seamless
flood, is not a stemming but a summoning
— flailing of adamant until it flow —
then standing up to the spate encounter
in the font — O crystal
blue-throated bird! — clear font of names?

Voir le dessous des cartes.
Thumbing motives. Ought one to stick pins
through such florid falsettos?
Dog-ear some metropolitan tag, then? Call down
for a new deck: love in hotels or Fords or cheaper
standing into doorways — lily of city lips,
Queen of Pique.
Of form and unity's fossil (a species), uniformity
(of order) is anamorphosis, disorder slicked down
over our love that fed among the lilies.

Indifferent under tossed confetti of stars,
what celebrant avails us comprehensive vault?
Squint up from under goaded covetings
of hubris into the babyblue where a bustard
publicizes cupid bows. Beneath him bristle
disciplined ranks of castor beans.
Toi qui soulages ta tripe — that was how he shaped
decorum, Mallarmé, to outhouse tribesmen *tripe*,
Tu peux dans cet acte obscur
Chanter ou fumer la pipe
Sans mettre des doigts au mur.
Shocked in the thick of cymbals,
drums pertaining to neither order
abutting on any adventure's total flux,
Zagreus is reborn to scare the children.
They daubed his infancy with slime, with toys
practiced upon it; astir to a rending,
dandled him up to a mirror. Where
and when beheld, where
was that seeming summer crowding sail?
You know the Mississippi? It oozes
over De Soto, sucks at his log and
does not know itself. Prime growth on the banks
is hard come by, hard to come by clouds
on water calcimined with condoms, burst clouds
sure to be snagged out on tips of hazel wands
by swindled kids. Hankering after
intimations from the underworld,
eyes glassed out, they trace
their geniture to bottom fish.
Grown up is the lad with the heart-shaped lips,
Car ma communion première
est bien passé.
     Ritual; but floribund
in rubble-choked chancre, a
         form projected,
intercepted sooner than space can round it,
surround it with retentive tenor; sibilation,
stanched, of hallucinated ghosts,
psycho-phantic, faces no sooner scrubbed

than tying tin cans to bitches' tails.
And in any ditch —

Fierce the onslaught,
impartial, inhuman; dialectic
and atom split
lacking unity of moral purpose. Thumbing through
the poet Fernando Pessoa, I found him
whetted on the congeries of four faces,
three stained wax, the other marble
fractured into standing helpless by
while warfare wheedles his muse with lies
and rapes her grace
with the local truth of twofold pains he had;
Fernando Pessoa betrayed to glittering surfaces
by categories seemingly authentic,
order demanding uniformity
to fix the solipsism
predictably in the forcinghouse of prodigies.

Alongside the barbed wire fence, whores in a rabble
of milfoil and bird-convoking chickweed;
a little this side where peach trees
let loud summer mornings drop, plush,
a laden fragrance crouches in limp goblets
melting rouge with fretted gold toward the sun,
short-skirted lips
in parked cars — frailty, a pink
easily chanced to Tarzan-eyes
with ergot, kisses lost back down the highway.
Voir le dessous des cartes. She rammed
my scarf between her legs and cued me in:
Go get it — if you want it. And my cloth,
who will divine it? But my craft is
to divine and round it.

They grow in a draggletail row
alongside the fence
near the outhouse
                    lily of city lips.

A SHIELD AGAINST THE TRAMPLING FOE

The unicorn bred virtue for a light
to prick all darkness in a swarm of bees.
When Samson riddled sweetness hived in might
the garden turned the desert of its keys.

Wish-deep, it feeds through lilies' white-at-ease.
The incandescent flanks no appetite
could tangle in thorn are lapped by virginities.
The unicorn bred virtue for a light

'gainst Hydra horned, black bolt & red-tipped white,
while hooves on Orion tread Pasiphaë and seize
with "stupefying solipsism" the right
to prick all darkness in a swarm of bees.

Foul broods corruptible through communities
violate their convert acolyte
whose faith had ploughed the loose sand at his knees
when Samson riddled sweetness hived in might.

Westward enclosed (while natron dissects the night
in Mykerinos' mummy, as filigrees
wound seven withes all green but now too tight),
the garden turned the desert of its keys.

Still might pitiless gold with wrought dance tease
the seething till the couchant hours requite
virginity, fold might. Who sleep as these
start alive instinct with garden's delight:
          the unicorn bred vertu.

NOTES

UNCOLLECTED POEMS

TRIADIC NODE FOR TIM REYNOLDS' DIGESTION.   Cassiodorus (490-585) performed an inestimable service for posterity by establishing, at a time when Rome under the reign of Ostrogothic kings was threatened by barbarism, a monastery, the aim of which was to conserve Roman culture. Under his guidance, his monks copied pagan and Christian authors. St. Paulinus of Nola (353-431), son of the Praetorian Prefect in Gaul, had his education entrusted to Ausonius (see the author's poem, " J' "), and he was an ascetic devoted to the poor. Stock was an ardent, sometimes almost ferocious, cultural "environmentalist" and a sympathizer to outcasts.

WIND IN THE MIRROR.   Max Scheler (1874-1928), a philosopher initially influenced by Husserl, used the phenomenological approach in all his writings. A critic of Kant's formalistic ethics, he espoused, rather, a teleological ethics of value similar, some say, to British idealist utilitarianism, wherein our values come primarily from our feelings. Scheler builds on Pascal's "logic of the heart."

THE SPACE BETWEEN TWO BLADES OF GRASS MEETS AN INTRACTABLE EGO. The poet has attached a note to the manuscript: "This title is my triumph. It's a double image, like that Victorian vanity table that turns into a skull as you watch. Only this title changes while you read the poem, and then changes back again." Jonah, one of God's wayward prophets, is a comic figure of the Old Testament in that he inadvertently oscillates between intuition and the worst sophism. En route to Tarshish he calms the stormy sea by ordering he be cast overboard; is swallowed by the whale; regurgitated; given his tree, and then a second chance by God to prophesy against Nineveh. Pomona is the Goddess of Fruit; hence, of cashew-apples.

MITHRIDATES VI.   The Roman Empire's principal threat in Asia Minor, this last King of Pontus took his name from Mithra, the Indo-Iranian God of Light and the source of the final Oriental mystery cult to infiltrate the West. Mithridates, after a terrible defeat by the Romans, tried to poison himself, and, some claim, having failed, ordered his death at the hands of a mercenary, while others suggest his physician intuited the sovereign's wish and complied, in league with Mithridates' unspoken complicity.

THE MIRACLE OF THE ROSES.   A parable of Jewish guilt and Roman superstition, at the least.

SIGISMONDO MALATESTA BRINGS HIS FAVORITE PHILOSOPHER'S BONES TO ITALY. If Pound has mythologized this figure in *The Cantos*, Stock has narrowed and sharpened the focus on Malatesta's rivalry with Urbino.

GO AS PLAYED IN THE BEST CIRCLES, etc. The poet, a considerable go player himself, loved the game's paradox: that, in one's attempt to surround the opponent's stones with "nets" of one's own stones, he risked inadvertent entrapment by the opponent's "nets." Go originated in Japan and is, some argue, older than chess. While chess is inexorably a contest of unrelenting aggression, Go is more of a lesson in continual opening of the ranks to encompass the opponent's. P.S. Liddell, an excellent player, consistently annoyed the poet during their games, not only by talking continuously but often by beating him fair and square, which perhaps has bearing on the "cautionary" tone of the poem immediately following this one.

SIR JOHN MANDEVILLE AND I SAT UP LATE TALKING. The great traveler, the English Herodotus.

A VOYAGER TAKES PAUSE. Blaise Cendrars is a well-known twentieth-century French poet and fiction writer, a great traveler to odd places as in his *Dan Yak*, and, as such, a natural for the poet, himself one for exotic landscapes, to address.

INVISIBLE GOLDEN SECTIONS. "A golden section is a rectangle based on the proportions of 3:2. I've reproduced this proportion in the rhyme scheme of each stanza and also in the five stanzas: the first three stanzas have no rhyming oddness, but the fourth (introducing the 2 proportion) is a tour de force in that all its rhymes are absurdly trite. *Stanza I*– Reference to Ghiberti's marvelous sculpted bronze doors in Florence. One of them is of Adam's dream during the sleep when Eve was created (for a far different interpretation see "Adam Lay Ibounden" in my *Covenants*). Here Adam's immured in the door's timeless worlds of art & dream, he & Eve part of each other, but also separate, and the dream a sign of separation. Oneiric space is thought to be without perspective, to touch the dreamer on all sides. His dream is private, hence the woman cannot share. Also, the function of a door (going in and out) is denied in Adam, being part of the door and so immobilized. *Stanza II*– The actors shift radically to a widower & a widow & "you." The widower (for purposes of this poem a masculine principle) in being "public" is distinguished from the dream ("private" of st. I) and inherits emotion – "tears" – and is identified in line 3 with the intellect. Thus we have:

<u>Widower</u>	<u>Widow</u>
intellect ("mind's mazy motions")	emotion ("tears")
masculine principle	feminine principle
undreaming	dreaming
public	private
bereaved (separated from widow)	(separated from widower)
sees woman as dead	sees man as dead

Lines 1-4 are a cycle: emotion$\overset{1}{\rightarrow}$ intellect$\overset{2}{\rightarrow}$ emotion. This third step cannot have been known by the first because intellect transforms the materials with which it works. Line 5 is a still more radical shift, for widow & widower become you (unified in a person), which is dropped till first line of final stanza. The one farther step may be a return to intellect in the cycle, tho' in fact each step of cycle may be considered a self-isolation, estrangement; indeed, the core of this poem is a complaint against the separation of emotion & intellect. However, using "farther" instead of "further" forces a spatialized view of the line, too. It is, perhaps, reminiscent of that last, terrible, ironic line of "Adam Lay Ibounden" – and "you" is threatened with sheer physical isolation. *Stanza III* – Division now extends to inanimate objects, the furniture that widow & widower, in their roles of actual man & woman, might have owned in joint possession (implying some kind of divorce). This last is reinforced by legal jargon. But it is also emotional & mental furnishings. Such furniture should not have to opt for one or the other, or even concern itself with preoccupations of that sort. The unspoken word would be one of love or unification. The reduction of values from human beings to furniture is completed by mere legality. *Stanza IV* – Return to Adam & Eve of st. I. Lack of love characterizes this stanza. The pop rhymes suggest, by analogy with popular songs, the sorry state into which man-woman & intellect-emotion relations have fallen. Man's rib, Eve, sticks in his throat, like the unspoken word of st. III. Eve cannot see beyond the fog (this detail was suggested by Sue Owen's "Fog"). A paradigm is an abstract diagram, which is enough to represent the widow. This "water and land" have, of course, nothing to do with the "water & fire" of the six-pointed star. They are just the opposite: creation by means of separation: water from land and bird from beast, as in the beginning of *Genesis*. Nature, as manifested in seasonal & lunar cycles, makes us no promises that we'll know the unity of love. *Stanza V* – "You" returns on the scene in an image that repeats & somewhat extends the earlier appearance. You, the reader, are entitled to substitute yourself for "you." Division is now seen as the tempter, the serpent who caused the fall from grace. From the solitude of this division & isolation, disorder in emotions (frenzy) & intellect (meanings not understood) result. The penultimate line is something of a poser. The "I" first (and lastly) appears here, which, along with its ejaculatory style and compression of imagery, makes it emotionally dramatic, but this is confused with the intellection of its puns, so that confusion is mimed. The tempter and "I" are identified as partially identical, since we share the same breath; also, the holding of breath as manifestation of expectancy, i.e., what's going to happen next? The second clause of the line is the I's realization that he is: (1) fattened or stupefied with thieves, and (2) in close association (also identified as partially identical) with thieves. The thieves are interpretable as any epistemological or psychological function that steals from another function – or as any evil force (serpent, division between functions or man & woman, etc.). The last line simply says that the division of time into temporal units (i.e., minutes) does no more than reprieve us time after time, and thinly, too, as against the thickness of function stealing from function. Whereas st. III relies on legal imagery, st. V uses criminal imagery, and the two are not, of course, unconnected." – *R.S.*

GIORGIONE'S *TEMPEST.*   Statius (45-96) was one of the chief poets of Rome's Silver Age of poetry. His natural and unaffected tone was one of flattery toward the emperor and court figures. Statius, the author seems to say, would never write – surely not with empathy – of gypsies.

THE PINCH.   Beginning probably with William Empson's, the villanelle has come a long way from its emasculations by the Nineties poets of England. It has proven for many an excellent satirical vehicle.

NATIONAL ANTHEM.   Stock on occasion would claim Drummond as the greatest twentieth-century poet, but, like all poets, he loved to exaggerate, on occasion.

HAIKU.   Here, two actually; the second, a double haiku, for the customary transliteration of the form into English employs seventeen syllables only.

THE LAYING-OUT OF LAZARUS.   Eleazar, one of the sons of Aaron and a priest under Moses' aegis, was dressed in indescribably elaborate garments (see references in *Exodus* 28; *Leviticus* 10:6, and *Numbers* 20:28). In *Numbers* 31:41, Eleazar is given a heave-offering by Moses on Mount Hor at God's direction, but in view of the laying-out described in this poem, the author most probably meant the garments in his phrase "God-helped Eleazar" in the penultimate line. Nonetheless, the reader might conceivably wish to weigh the irony of Lazarus' rising as a heave-offering from God.

SOME SIGNS VISIBLE BEFORE JUDGMENT

WITH A MACHETE ACROSS MY KNEES. For Sato's sword see Yeats' "A Dialogue of Self and Soul," especially lines 9-16.

AZAZEL. In Hebrew legend Azazel is whatever receives, despoils and devours the scapegoat.

COVENANTS

(It is to be hoped that the year 1967 exacts no apology for the prose morsels that in less barbarous times accompanied poetry as a matter of course. However, I have observed a trend among the so-called *avant-garde* (*Everything changes − except the* avant-garde. −Valéry) to include its prose in the body or corpse of the poem. The few notes that follow are for the most part founded on questions asked by friends about the poems. I have tried to limit them to the minimum consistent with their appearance at all; that is, they make no attempt to exhaust or encircle any poem with explanation or facts. If some of the poems seem nevertheless obscure, lay it to the esteem in which I hold the reader.)

BALLADE TO BE READ IN THE MEDICI GARDENS. The Medici Gardens were traditionally placed at the disposal of apprentice artists for their training and delight. But Piero abused his power by forcing the young Michelangelo to pass an entire winter creating in the perishing material of snow.

TO TUI, etc. The pervading symbol of this elegy is the *irapurú* (ee-rah´poo-roo). This bird's fable (that its feather, obtained by specific rituals, brings good luck) has become familiar through Villa-Lobos' ballet, *Irapurú*, as well as through the film of the same name. But its reality, far more arresting and marvelous than the fable, and attested to by such stolidly scientific minds as Mme. Snethlage's, brings to bear upon its trance-inducing mating song. When this inconspicuous brown bird sings, animals of the most diverse and hostile sorts are attracted from miles around. Mme. Snethlage was herself so attracted upon one memorable occasion. All the creature-world is in perfect concord during the concert. What ensues on the song's cessation is, perhaps, the product of my own experience reflecting on the treaties and concords of my fellows. Bellbird, *Procneas carunculata*: the most strident of birds. Garimpeiro (gah´reem-pay´roo): Brazilian diamond or gold seeker. For the Blue Dragon, Vermilion Bird, Black Tortoise, and White Tiger see *The Natural Power of Things*, a chapter of Wang Ch'ung's *The Weight on the*

Balance: "Heaven, by emitting the essence of these four star clusters, produces the bodies of the four animals on earth" (translated by Chao Tze-Chiang in his version of the *I Ching*).

STUDY OF A HOUSE WITH GARDEN ATTACHED. The moral: take the lissome maid and let the upholstered mistress go. Quixaba (kee-sha´ ba), *Bumelia sertorum*: a Brazilian fruit, brilliantly black and much like the small plum in size and shape, but superior in flavor. The *blue flower* is the all-suffusing romantic symbol in Novalis' *Heinrich von Ofterdingen*.

THE POET MÁRIO FAUSTINO, etc. Having fallen out of intelligence with my friends in Belém, Brazil, I did not hear of Mário's death until 1965, three years after the great tragedy to Brazilian poetry. *The Man and His Hour (O Homen e sua Hora)* is the title of one of his books. Carlos Drummond de Andrade is, in my opinion, the greatest of living poets; but Mário Faustino digged in as deep a mine, and the ore he scattered over his shoulder blinded Apollo by day and a pilot by night.

THE SYNAPSE. Erato is the muse of erotic, Polyhymnia of sacred and Clio of historical (or, as we might say today, social) poetry.

POEM ON HOLY SATURDAY. I have borrowed that luminous line with which Coleridge kenspeckles *The Rime's* turning point or moment of the blessing bestowed.

APPENDIX: SOME EARLY POEMS

THE DANCE. The second indented section, beginning with line 71, is in part a paraphrase of the *XXVIIth Ode of Solomon*.

VISITATION. Bathylites are former mountain bases which have been pushed up into the crowning position, usually forming a sort of vault over the mountain.

IN TRANSFORMATION OF AN IMAGO. Sometimes the story goes that Helen was never in Troy at all. It is a fascinating story and may be found in Apollodorus (*Epitome* iii.5). The charming tale is told by Stesichorus (in the fragments cited by John Tzetzes in *On the Cassandra of Lycophron* 113), Plato (*Phaedrus* 243 A) and Pausanius (iii.19,13), of how Stesichorus was blinded for defaming Helen in a poem, but regained his sight upon writing the palinode in which he asserted that only her simulacrum had been carried off to Troy, whereas Helen in the flesh was abducted by Hermes and put in the care of Hermes, King of Egypt. In Porphyry's *De Antro Nympharum*, the description of the Cave of the Nereids in the *Odyssey* (xiii. 109-112) is interpreted as an allegory of the universe. Poseidon was also known as Poseidon Hippios and from earliest times was associated with horses; but his presence in a Cave of the Nymphs is also plausible, since he was also styled Nymphagetes. Athena's name means "without mother's milk." When Pallas the Titan tried to woo her, Athena slew him and added his name to her own as a warning to other suitors.

THE WANDERING JEW AND THE HEAVENLY HOSTS. *Part I*: his situation in the world of space, time and history. *Part II*: his meditation on the constellations. On the analogy of Ahasuerus' spatial situation, which can perceive all the constellations at once, I have assumed freedom of movement not only between astronomy and astrology, but also between the astrologies of various cultures, hoping, among other things, to encourage a syncretism. Is not Pound's treatment of history of a similar nature? The philosopher is Berdyaev, one of the few aching philosophers who did not ache for the sake of the ache.

INSCRIPTION FOR A TEMPLE OF CLOACINA. The great twentieth-century Portuguese poet, Fernando Pessoa, created five distinct *heteronymos* (as he called them), each with a separate body of poetry written in a separate style (ranging from Whitmanesque to the Horation ode as it is understood on the Continent), each with a separate biography. Tarzan-eyes: that is to say, they swing from limb to limb.

A SHIELD AGAINST THE TRAMPLING FOE. Only a virgin's lap can lure a unicorn into captivity. In Annunciation paintings and tapestries, he is often associated with the Enclosed Garden in which Mary must meet the male Annunciator. The colors of his horn are white, black and red, which are also the colors of the sardonyx, symbol of virgin gestation. Monocerus, the unicorn panoplied in the Southern heavens, is so situated that his horn points to Hydra and his hooves trample on Orion. The quotation of stanza III is from the *De Naturae Planctu* of Alanus Insulis, the entire phrase reading thus: "Pasiphaë committed a stupefying solipsism with the bull." Alanus, a scholastic of the realist persuasion as well as a poet, with this phrase makes more sense of the Middle Ages then Huizinga and his like are able to do in volume after volume. Mykerinos: because the solar bee emblem was first found in his tomb.